WRITTEN IN TEARS

WRITTEN IN TEARS

A GRIEVING FATHER'S JOURNEY THROUGH PSALM 103

LUKE VELDT

DISCOVERY HOUSE
PUBLISHERS®

Discovery House Publishers is affiliated with RBC Ministries,
Grand Rapids, Michigan.

Discovery House books are distributed to the trade exclusively by
Barbour Publishing, Inc., Uhrichsville, Ohio.

Requests for permission to quote from this book should be directed to:
Permissions Department, Discovery House Publishers, P.O. Box 3566,
Grand Rapids, MI 49501.

Library of Congress Cataloging-in-Publication Data
Veldt, Luke,
    Written in tears : a grieving father's journey through Psalm 103 /
Luke Veldt.
        p.   cm.
    Includes bibliographical references and index.
    ISBN 978-1-57293-382-8 (alk. paper)
    1. Consolation. 2. Veldt, Luke, 1961– 3. Children—
Death—Religious aspects—Christianity. 4. Bible. O.T. Psalms
CIII—Criticism, interpretation, etc. 5. Suffering—Religious
aspects—Christianity. I. Veldt, Allison, d. 2006 Death and burial.
II. Title.
    BV4907.V46 2010
    248.8'66—dc22   2010020609

PRINTED IN THE UNITED STATES OF AMERICA

10 11 12 13 14 /10 9 8 7 6 5 4 3 2 1

CONTENTS

I sometimes hold it half a sin
  To put in words the grief I feel;
  For words, like Nature, half reveal
And half conceal the Soul within . . .

In words, like weeds, I'll wrap me o'er,
  Like coarsest clothes against the cold:
  But that large grief which these enfold
Is given in outline and no more.

One writes, that 'Other friends remain,'
  That 'Loss is common to the race'—
  And common is the commonplace,
And vacant chaff well meant for grain.

That loss is common would not make
  My own less bitter, rather more:
  Too common! Never morning wore
To evening, but some heart did break.

Alfred, Lord Tennyson,
from *In Memoriam A. H. H.*

Acknowledgments

NEAR THE END OF THIS BOOK, I TALK ABOUT JACOB'S struggle with God, a struggle that defined and transformed his life. That struggle has been duplicated countless times through the years—the desperate, draining strivings; the agonizing process of letting go of old habits and perspective; the new identity and new faith. In my own struggle, I owe a great deal to those who have struggled both before me and along with me.

As tragedy is a surprise, so too is this: the discovery that the refining process you are enduring—the fight, the new perspective—is not new with you. Or rather, it is new with you in the same way it is new with everyone else who has ever suffered. Those who write about what they have suffered often end up saying much the same thing. Some say it haltingly, some confidently, some movingly—but all *personally*. It's as if the discovery of the light bulb were repeated over and over, with none of the inventors ever borrowing from the work of the others. The discovery is always original, always costly, always enlightening. We've all experienced it, that comic book moment when the light bulb goes on over our heads; it would be comical, too, if it weren't of such vital importance in each of our lives.

So I find in books written by fellow sufferers that the things I discovered have been discovered by many others as well. All speak of the fight, of questioning everything they ever believed, of dissatisfaction with easy answers. All speak of a new identity, of lives suddenly and permanently transformed. All speak of things learned and gained at terrible cost.

Yet I feel compelled to tell my own story, though I now understand that it's not as terribly unique as I first thought. I'm a discoverer of the North Pole who, after frostbite and windstorms and discouragement and eating his sled dogs, reaches his goal and finds that it has been discovered thousands of times before—yet finds his own journey no less valuable because of its commonness. Or, more accurately, I have not yet reached the goal and probably never will; but on the way, I must share what I've found and hope it will encourage others in their trek as I've been encouraged myself.

I owe special thanks to those friends who allowed me to include their stories in these pages—to Kevin and Kay Ann, John and Lynn, Carmen. If this book proves to be of any value, they get much of the credit.

Those who know our family will be surprised that I do not also talk about the experiences of my brother Matt and his wife Molly, who lost three of their own children to a rare genetic disorder. Their story would make compelling reading, but I can't write it; it humbles me into silence. Besides, their story couldn't be told in a book without taking over the book completely. One day they'll have to tell that story themselves.

Thanks to my cousin Susan, to my father, and to other friends and family members who offered proofreading help and suggestions. Thanks, too, to Warren and Betty Wiersbe, whose daily prayers for me and for this book were a great encouragement.

To those friends and even strangers who prayed for us in the first few days, weeks, and months after Allison's death, our entire family owes our eternal gratitude. I have no way of measuring your impact on our lives, but I know that your prayers were crucial. Thank you so much.

My wife Jodi and my children deserve a medal for their patience with me. They all miss Allison as much as I do, and in unique ways. Though their feelings are not exactly mine, they've had to listen to my perspective over and over again, first in countless Bible studies and sermons about grief and Psalm 103 and now in this book. If they have ever gotten tired of it, they have kept it to themselves. I'm very grateful for them and proud of them all.

Finally, I owe more than I can express to a group of young people from four countries who spent a lot of time hanging around our house and forcing their way into our hearts in the year following Allison's death. Many of the ideas about Psalm 103 presented in this book were first tried out in a Bible study with these young people, and it was with them that we started to see that perhaps God would not allow our suffering to be wasted. Luccas, Jessica, Alexandros, Erica, Emily: May you all be blessed with an intense desire to follow God all your days. You will always be an important part of our family. Come home and visit sometime.

Introduction

SUNDAY, AUGUST 27, 2006. THE SUN BEATS DOWN steadily but not oppressively on the streets of Pamplona. It's a lazy Sunday afternoon in Spain, the kind of day siestas were made for.

The traffic on the streets—if you can call the occasional car "traffic"—is also lazy, relaxed and unhurried, with one exception. A silver van speeds down the avenue, pausing only briefly before shooting through a red light.

In the back of the van a young girl is spread out across the seat, her head cradled in her mother's arms. "I need you to breathe, Allison!" the woman says. "Keep breathing!" But Allison *is* breathing, the deep breathing that's past sleep, the coma from which she will not wake up. Or perhaps she has already awakened; perhaps, somewhere between the house and the hospital, her soul slipped away from the presence of her panicked parents and into the calm presence of her Father.

The sun shines on a lazy afternoon in Pamplona as the girl's parents speed down the road toward the end of their world.

CHAPTER 1

PRECIOUS IN THE SIGHT OF THE LORD: THE FATHER'S EMBRACE

OUR DAUGHTER ALLISON DIED OF A MASSIVE BRAIN hemorrhage, caused by a condition she had—unknown to us—from birth. A cerebral malformation such as Allison's (the surgeon explained to us later) invariably leads to hemorrhage, often fatal. Sometimes the hemorrhage is triggered by a blow to the head or by physical exercise; sometimes, as in Alli's case, it is seemingly not triggered by anything.

We had no warning. Allison was, as far as we could see, a normal, healthy thirteen-year-old, active and happy. She helped teach a Sunday school lesson about heaven that morning. When we came home from church, the rest of us went to our rooms upstairs to change into comfortable clothes while Allison stayed downstairs to get her little sister something to eat. Shortly after, she cried out for help. We found her slumped over the table; her words were slurred as she told us that her legs were numb, that she couldn't lift her head. Was she in pain? No. Had she eaten something? No. Perhaps a cool cloth on her forehead—but then she passed out.

We had her at the hospital within fifteen minutes. A flurry of activity; an anxious wait in the hall; a conference with a nurse. Allison's pupils, the nurse said, were already completely dilated when she arrived at the hospital, an ominous sign. They were taking Allison to the hospital across the street for an emergency operation; the hospitals were connected by a tunnel, and we could walk with them.

The surgeon spoke with us there. The situation couldn't be worse, he said. He frankly didn't believe an operation would help, but he would operate anyway—sometimes the bodies of the young do surprising things, so they give them every chance to perform a miracle on themselves. . . .

The rest was waiting. After the operation, Allison was on life support; it wasn't inconceivable that she would recover, but it was unlikely. Her older brother and sister, Nate and Amber, came to the hospital late in the afternoon to see Allison and tell her goodbye. A doctor asked us for a conference and carefully broached the subject of organ donation. And we waited.

People from our church came and waited with us. Neighbors and friends stayed with our other children. Our friends and family around the world prayed. At my parents' church in the United States, the planned service was scrapped and replaced with an hour of prayer.

A friend called from Romania that night. "She's gone," I told him.

⌒

The next few days were a blur: talking to doctors, planning the memorial service, meeting family members at the airport. Crying, praying, remembering. Trying to sleep. Consoling our kids. Wondering whether anything in the world made any sense.

Jodi and I are Christians, from Christian families. Since we were young, our goal has been to learn about Jesus Christ, to live in a way that would reflect His presence in us, and to share our faith with others. We each have spent more than forty years in that life—attending church, listening to sermons, studying the Bible. Before moving to Spain, we worked for ten years as missionaries in Romania. We have watched God take care of us in all sorts of difficult circumstances.

Yet on one of those first nights after Allison's death, as we were alone in our bedroom, Jodi asked me through her tears, "Is it all true? Is any of it true? Is there a God, and is Alli with Him? Oh, it needs to be true."

I had no answer; I had been feeling exactly the same myself. Forty years of faith, distilled in this moment to a single paralyzing thought: Is any of it true? Is there really a God? Or is this the way faith began, with hurting people who invented a God they desperately needed?

My doubt caught me by surprise. There is no promise in the message of Jesus Christ that His followers are exempt from suffering; on the contrary, the Bible advises us that God's people can expect to suffer. And it's not as if I were unacquainted with death, even the death of children. I've cried with and comforted others who have suffered that kind of loss and had my faith strengthened as I saw God's presence in their lives. So as terrible as the death of a child is, objectively speaking it should not have challenged my faith.

But there was nothing objective about the death of this child. This child was Allison, our own Allison. And losing her somehow changed everything.

⟀

Allison was the fourth of six children. Each of those children is priceless, each unique; why does Allison now seem to stand out from the rest? We know that she wasn't perfect, but it's hard for us now to think of any meaningful way in which she wasn't. Her life seems to us like a cut jewel, exquisite from whichever way we look at it. Perhaps it's just a trick of memory that now makes Allison seem so special. It doesn't feel like a trick, though; it feels like having your eyes opened to the plain truth. It's as if her death has cut and polished our perspective so that we can see her accurately for the first time.

Allison, more than anyone else I know, had the gift of appreciating the moment. She loved making friends, giving back rubs and foot massages, spending money, making things out of beads and glue and string, and fishing with her dad. I think Allison probably came as close as anybody could to living each day without any regrets.

Somehow, no matter where Allison was, it seemed she was always surrounded by all of her favorite people.

She smiled easily and gave bone-crushing hugs.

She loved to help out. If the family was watching television and I asked if someone would go to the kitchen and get their lazy father a drink, the other kids barely had time to hold their breath and try to look invisible before Alli jumped up and said, "Sure!"

Allison had an intuitive and uncommon sense of what's important. She liked to play games, but she didn't care about keeping score. She never showed any indications of trying to be the smartest person in the room, or of caring who was. When given the choice of spending fifteen minutes on chores or an hour taking care of her little sister Andrea, she always chose the time with her sister.

Allison was best friend to Andrea, who has Down syndrome. "What's going to happen to Andrea when I die?" Jodi would occasionally fret, and Allison would always respond, "Don't worry about that, Mom! When I grow up, Andy can live with me!"

She was best friend to her little brother Nick and spent more time with him and Andrea than she did with her older siblings, though she was closer to their ages than his. (Nick was four years younger than Alli; Nate, Amber, and Anna were two, three, and five years older.)

She was best friend to her sister Amber, a friend Amber could confide in and not compete with.

She was best friend to her cousin Kendra and her friend Breanna (with whom she had contrived intricate plans about how they were going to spend the rest of their lives together). Another of Allison's stateside friends, before having heard of Allison's death, described Allison in a school assignment as one of the people who had most influenced her life. A lot of us would now say the same.

Allison was also best friend to two classmates in Pamplona. Adjusting to a new school while learning a new language was a challenge for Alli, as it was for all of our kids. But she was soon friends with all the girls in the class and planned to invite them all for a big birthday party in February. "This will be so much fun!" said the class's most popular girls. "But don't invite *them*," they said, pointing out two classmates. "Nobody likes them."

"Of course I'll invite them," said Allison. "They're my friends like everybody else. Everyone's invited."

"Well, if they come, we're not coming."

And that's how Allison came to celebrate her thirteenth birthday with two friends and enough food for fifteen. That, too, is how there came to be three unpopular girls in the class for the rest of the year instead of two.

After the party, Jodi asked Allison if she felt bad about the girls who didn't come, if inviting these two friends had been worth it. "Oh, yes!" said Allison, her eyes shining. "We had the best time ever!"

That was Allison.

She did feel bad about the friends she lost that day, and it was hard for Jodi and me to see the frustrations she faced at school in the following months. But we're so glad now that she did the right thing. We're so proud of her.

We miss her so much. It's hard to imagine how we'll be able to go on without her.

SOMETIMES I THINK THAT happiness is over for me. I look at photos of the past and immediately comes the thought: that's when we were still happy. But I can still laugh, so I guess that isn't quite it. Perhaps what's over is happiness as the fundamental tone of my existence. Now sorrow is that.

Sorrow is no longer the islands but the sea.

Nicholas Wolterstorff, *Lament for a Son*[1]

Within a few days after Allison's death we were weary, and weariness soon became our normal state. We had a hard time sleeping at night—and an even harder time finding a reason to get out of bed in the morning. We had no energy for some of the simplest tasks and little motivation to attempt major projects.

You've heard people who suffer great loss compare the experience to a punch in the stomach or a kick in the head. You've heard it so often you don't hear it anymore. It's lost its impact; it's a cliché. Yet I can't describe our emotional state better than to say that each morning, one second after we awoke, we had the wind knocked out of us by the thought, "It wasn't a dream. Alli is gone." It *is* like a kick in the head. It knocks you off balance; it takes away your desire to move on.

We didn't wish we were dead, but we didn't really care if we kept on living, either.

---

1. Nicholas Wolterstorff, *Lament for a Son* (Grand Rapids: William B. Eerdmans, 1987), 47.

Despite my newfound doubt, the first place I looked for answers to my questions and comfort for my grief was the Bible. This makes sense if you consider the Bible a supernatural book. Where better to turn in times of trial and doubt if not to the Word of God?

If, on the other hand, you think that the Bible is just one of man's many feeble attempts to search for God or to create Him after his own image, you may find it incomprehensible that I was turning to it even as I was asking myself whether any of it was true. Remember, though, that the Bible was for me the most natural place to look for answers. And I didn't want to reject it blindly any more than I wanted to accept it blindly.

I didn't really want to reject it at all. But easy answers didn't appeal to me either. Allison was gone. What does the Bible really say about that? Are the answers it offers authentic, trustworthy? I knew that a drowning man will grasp at anything that looks like a lifeline; I wanted to be sure that the one to which I was clinging was the real thing. And so I read the Bible, more thoughtfully than ever before.

As I had been surprised by my doubt, I was surprised now by what I found in the Bible—not one surprise, but a series of surprises.

I was surprised to find how directly the authors of the Bible spoke to my own situation. These weren't detached philosophers and theologians; they were real men who struggled with real doubts and pain, as I had. I found in these men a community of fellow sufferers.

I was surprised that I had never seen that before.

I was surprised to find that I was learning more about God in my sorrow than I ever had in times of joy. "The Bible was written in tears," said A. W. Tozer, "and to tears it will reveal its best treasures."[2]

And I was surprised to realize how many wrong assumptions about God I had to unlearn.

~

One of my first surprises in the days after Alli's death came from Psalm 103, a psalm of King David. David knew what it was like to be in the pit. He not only lost three of his children, he also shouldered the burden of knowing that he was at least partly responsible for each of their deaths (more on that later). Here, halfway through Psalm 103, David describes God's love:

> . . . as the heavens are high above the earth,
> so great is his steadfast love toward those who
>   fear him;
> as far as the east is from the west,
>   so far he removes our transgressions from
>   us.
> As a father has compassion for his children,
>   so the Lord has compassion for those who
>   fear him.
> For he knows how we were made;
>   he remembers that we are dust (vv. 11–14).

When I had read this psalm in the past, I had always noticed two illustrations here for the infinite nature of God's love: the distance between heaven and earth and the distance from east to west. Now, though, it occurred to me that the next line of the psalm—"As a father has compassion for his children"—is

---

2. *Best of A.W. Tozer*, comp. Warren W. Wiersbe (Baker Book House, 1978), 61. Originally in *God Tells the Man Who Cares*.

not the start of a new paragraph or idea but is, in fact, the third in the series of images. As the last item on the list, it's the most important, the one the others lead up to; it's the most familiar and yet the most dramatic expression of God's limitless love.

"As a father has compassion for his children." As I read this, I was struck by the implication that God shares my grief. My thoughts about Allison are His thoughts. He loves her, too, even more than I do. He gave her special personality to her; having given her life, He now mourns her death.

God is in this with me. He is not aloof, detached, controlling everything from afar, untouched by His own decisions. He doesn't say, "You've got to suffer—never mind why." He is deeply involved, personally affected. "Precious in the sight of the Lord is the death of his saints," another psalm tells us.[3]

And he knows how I feel right now. God knows what it's like for a father to see his child die. "My God, my God, why have you forsaken me?" Jesus cried from the cross, and His Father heard and did nothing. I've heard a lot of sermons that emphasize the price Jesus paid on the cross, totally separated from and abandoned by God; I don't know that I've heard any that focus on what it cost the Father to turn from His Son.

How could He do it? I wondered. *How could He hear His child cry for help and not respond?* The words of John 3:16, a verse I've known by heart since I was three years old, now spoke to me in a new way: "For God so loved the world that he gave his only Son . . ." I had never before understood so clearly what God's love for the world cost Him. "God's love was revealed among us in this way: God sent his only Son into the world so that we might live through him. In this is love, not that we loved God but that he loved us and sent his Son to be the atoning sacrifice for our sins."[4]

---

3. Psalm 116:15 NIV
4. 1 John 4:9–10

As high as the heavens above the earth, as far as east from west, as profound as a father's love for his children.

It took the death of my daughter for me to begin to understand the love of God.

～

This insight into God's compassion didn't answer all my questions. I found it to be a comfort, though, and looking back now, it seems to me that the comfort I received was far more meaningful than any answer could have been. Because at that point in our grief, we didn't really want answers. We wanted Allison back. Answers, even if I could get them, would not dispel my grief; answers are a poor substitute for a daughter.

THE QUESTION THAT KEEPS coming to all of us is 'Why?' . . . But this I know: even if we could explain why (Allison) left us, the explanation wouldn't begin to heal our broken hearts.

Warren W. Wiersbe and David W. Wiersbe,
Comforting the Bereaved[5]

It wasn't an answer we were lacking, but a presence, a person. And you can't replace a person with a doctrine. So the presence of God, while not the presence we were craving, was the right sort of response. It was more a hug than a word of wisdom. And as in the case of all of those struck with grief, a hug was what we needed most.

Every day, I struggled to deal with a world without Allison. As I struggled, I began to read Psalm 103 daily. And each day—or nearly so—I noticed something that I had never seen there before. The more I read and reflected over what I read,

---

5. Warren W. Wiersbe and David W. Wiersbe, *Comforting the Bereaved* (Chicago: Moody Press, 1985), 86.

the more I learned about God and about life. And the things I learned helped me to get from one day to another.

I read Psalm 103 nearly every day for over a year.

You should be warned in advance that none of the things I learned prove the existence of God or fully explain the problem of suffering.

None of the things I learned dispelled my sorrow. This book is not about how I got through grief, how I got over the loss of Allison and went on to lead a normal life. Sorrow is my normal life now. We still grieve; two years after Allison's death, we still don't sleep well. You don't get over the loss of a child—ever. Nor would I want to. My grief reminds me that Allison was important, and losing her an irreplaceable loss.

This book is about how I came to know God better, not just despite my loss, but because of it. It's written in the hope that the things I learned and the comfort I experienced will be of help in your life as well.

PSALM 103

Bless the Lord, O my soul,
   and all that is within me,
   bless his holy name.
Bless the Lord, O my soul,
   and do not forget all his benefits—
who forgives all your iniquity,
   who heals all your diseases,
who redeems your life from the Pit,
   who crowns you with steadfast love and mercy,
who satisfies you with good as long as you live
   so that your youth is renewed like the eagle's.

The Lord works vindication
   and justice for all who are oppressed.
He made known his ways to Moses,
   his acts to the people of Israel.
The Lord is merciful and gracious,
   slow to anger and abounding in steadfast love.
He will not always accuse,
   nor will he keep his anger forever.
He does not deal with us according to our sins,
   nor repay us according to our iniquities.
For as the heavens are high above the earth,
   so great is his steadfast love toward those who
   fear him;
as far as the east is from the west,
   so far he removes our transgressions from us.

As a father has compassion for his children,
  so the Lord has compassion for those who fear
    him.
For he knows how we were made;
  he remembers that we are dust.

As for mortals, their days are like grass;
  they flourish like a flower of the field;
for the wind passes over it, and it is gone,
  and its place knows it no more.
But the steadfast love of the Lord is from everlasting
  to everlasting
    on those who fear him,
    and his righteousness to children's children,
to those who keep his covenant
  and remember to do his commandments.

The Lord has established his throne in the heavens,
  and his kingdom rules over all.
Bless the Lord, O you his angels,
  you mighty ones who do his bidding,
    obedient to his spoken word.
Bless the Lord, all his hosts,
  his ministers that do his will.
Bless the Lord, all his works,
  in all places of his dominion.
Bless the Lord, O my soul.

CHAPTER 2

SACRIFICE OF PRAISE: ALIGNING YOURSELF WITH GOD

"BLESS THE LORD, O MY SOUL," BEGINS PSALM 103. "And all that is within me, bless his holy name."

It's easy enough to follow this advice in good times. It's harder to bless the Lord when your world has been shattered, when you feel that you've been stripped of all your blessings. When the "all that is within" you includes frustrations, doubt, anger. When it includes tears.

There are some things I can't talk about now without tears coming. And while crying doesn't embarrass me anymore, it does tend to put a crimp in conversation. So there are certain things that I know better than to try to talk about. Every once in awhile, I discover new things that fit into that category.

I know, for example, that I can't describe to you what it means to me that my father's church replaced their planned Sunday morning service with a time of extended prayer for us on the day that Allison died.

And I found out recently that when some new acquaintances tell me that their daughter just had a baby and named her Allison, I'm unable to say, as I'd like to, "Nice name." Or anything else.

And I have a hard time talking about the picture on our wall.

I'll get back to the picture on the wall, but let me give you a little background first.

Allison and I loved to fish together. I have pictures of us with beautiful catches of bluegill, perch, and pike. On one of our more successful outings, we hiked together to my secret spot at a lake in the backwoods of Upper Michigan and walked back out with our limit of largemouth bass.

On one vacation when Allison was young, I left her at the cabin while I was out fishing with one or two of the other kids. She surprised herself by catching two small fish from shore all by herself. "I can't wait to show Dad!" she gushed. "This is the best day of my life!"

Here's the point: Allison barely cared about fishing. She just loved being with her dad.

She loved it so much that one early morning of a cold Michigan spring, with the snow still on the ground, she insisted on accompanying me to the White River to try our luck on steelhead. I tried to talk her out of it. It was going to be very cold, and fishing for steelhead isn't easy, and I didn't even know if there were any out there yet. But she wouldn't be put off.

It was still dark when we arrived at the river. We waded into the frigid water together and shivered as we fished. Ice kept forming in the eyes of the fly rod. It didn't take very long for Allison to decide that she had made a mistake: she was freezing; her hands were numb (though she was wearing gloves); she wanted to go home. But home was far away, and I wasn't willing to give up the morning's fishing.

"I can do one thing for you," I told her. "Take off your gloves. Then put your hands down my shirtfront, past my neck, inside all four layers of clothing, and hold them tight against my chest." She did it. I screamed. I'll never forget the sensation of those blocks of ice melting into my skin or her delighted laughter as I suffered and she got warm.

I don't think we caught any fish that day. We did much better in the fall on trips targeting spawning salmon. I caught several while I was with her, and she enjoyed the experience of fighting some as well. We were never quite able to get one of her fish to the net, though. We were a little disappointed, but only a little. We knew—we thought—that there was a lot of fishing and a lot of salmon in our future.

Those times we had together are very special to me now. When Allison died, I considered finding a good artist to paint a picture of the two of us fishing together. I could provide pictures of Allison and the White and let the artist work from there.

And then, before I could commission the picture, I found it offered for sale.

Or rather, I found for sale a print of an oil painting by the artist G. Harvey that was almost exactly what I had in mind. It shows a man and his young daughter (or son—a baseball cap on the youngster's head allows for either possibility) fishing together on a river that looks a lot like the White. A few of the details in the picture don't fit us exactly—I don't wear a cowboy hat and we never brought a dog along—but I knew it was the picture I was looking for when I saw the title: *In My Father's Presence.*

Yes, in her Father's presence. That's exactly where Allison is now, experiencing the kind of pleasure we had together, only infinitely more.

I hope. I believe. I know. I think. That hope is my anchor, the one certainty in an unsure world; it's the huge gamble on which I've staked my life. Some days I'm as sure of it as I am of the ground I'm standing on. On other days, I wonder if I'm just trying to talk myself into something.

I think maybe Peter would understand how I feel. "Will you leave me too?" Jesus asked the Twelve one day when many of His disciples were forsaking Him because of His difficult teachings. "Where would we go, Lord?" replied Peter. "You have the words of eternal life. We have come to believe and know that you are the Holy One of God."[6]

Peter's confession is a rock-solid declaration of faith—or perhaps much less. Perhaps what Peter is saying is, "Where would we go, Lord? You're the best thing out there, and frankly there aren't all that many options. Who else is offering us eternal life? Following you, the world makes sense, even though there's so little that I fully understand. You have to be the Son of God. Our lives our invested in you; it has to be true!"

Maybe Peter is whistling in the graveyard, or yelling—yelling out his faith in order to drown out the voice of the mourners or to drown out his own doubts. It seems certain that he didn't understand Jesus' difficult teachings any more than those who left Jesus did. Maybe he believed not because he was sure, but because the alternative was unthinkable.

Some days—not all, but some—that's as far as I'm able to go. I stand in front of the picture and I think, *That's the way it has to be. Either Allison really is in her Father's presence, enjoying Him and herself to an impossibly wonderful extent—or nothing in the whole world has any meaning or importance.*

This, strangely enough, is a comfort. Because I feel that there *is* sense in the world, that there is, ultimately, purpose and meaning to Allison's life, and to mine. I wouldn't know how to deny that if I wanted to. And if there's not a person who loves me behind that purpose and meaning, where would I go?

---

6.   John 6:69

And so I bless the Lord, even as I hurt, even as I question God. In doing so, I become part of a long tradition.

There is a passage of Scripture from early in Israel's history (shortly after God sent Moses to lead the Israelites out of slavery in Egypt) that is of signal importance to the chosen people of God. It was so important, in fact, that they were to keep it literally in front of their faces each day: carved in their doorposts and gates; bound on their hands and foreheads; recited to their children at home and away, when they lay down and when they rose up:

> "Hear, O Israel: The LORD is our God, the LORD alone. You shall love the LORD your God with all your heart, and with all your soul, and with all your might."[7]

Given the prominence of these verses in the life and beliefs of the Jews, it's hard to imagine that David did not have it in mind when he wrote, "Bless the Lord, O my soul, and all that is within me, bless his holy name."

David understood that blessing the Lord halfway is not only undesirable, it's impossible. You can't truly bless the Lord with half of your being any more than you can swim with half of your body. Blessing Him halfway is holding on to the side of the pool and doing a lot of splashing. You have to bless God with heart, soul, might, and everything you have, or not at all.

If I'm going to bless the Lord with all that is in me, my blessing will consist of a lot of gratitude for the good things I've experienced in my life. But it is also going to include some doubt, some uncertainty, and a lot of sadness.

I think David's blessing was formed out of much the same sort of stuff.

---

7. Deuteronomy 6:4–5

The world of the Psalms is charged with emotion: joy, sorrow, triumph, despair, repentance, anger, exultation. Any intense emotion—even an intensely personal emotion—is fitting material for the psalmist's song.

Of the 150 psalms, Psalm 103 is the most intensely personal, the most introspective. While other psalms are addressed to the people of God ("O sing to the Lord" [96] or, "Let us sing to the Lord" [95]) or to God ("to you, O Lord, I will sing" [101]), only Psalm 103 is addressed primarily to the psalmist himself. "Bless the Lord, O my soul," David tells himself, "and do not forget all his benefits."

I think it's important to note that David does not begin his psalm by blessing the Lord, but rather by urging himself to bless the Lord. Why would he do that? If he feels like blessing the Lord, why not just do it instead of telling himself to do it? There are many psalms in which he does just that. Perhaps, though, he doesn't feel like blessing God; perhaps that's just the point.

I can think of only two situations in which we might have to remind ourselves to bless the Lord. The first is when things are going so well for us that we are in danger of taking our happiness for granted, of forgetting that God is its source. We see this sort of reminder in Deuteronomy 6:10–12 (immediately following the mandate to love God with all your heart, soul, and strength), which says, in effect, "When God brings you into the land He's promised you and gives you all sorts of good things you haven't worked for and life is good and easy, take care not to forget the One who provided you with all of those blessings."

The second situation is the exact opposite: it's when things are going so badly that the last thing we would naturally do is bless the Lord. When we've suffered an unthinkable tragedy.

Our spouse tells us they're in love with someone else.

Or we're hurt deeply by a friend.

Or our child dies.

At times like these, our troubles loom so large that they're all we see. We tend to forget past joys entirely and to become oblivious to present blessings.

Psalm 103 speaks to this kind of experience. It's sometimes mistaken for a spontaneous outpouring of thanks to God, but it's much more than that. It is a *deliberate* response of blessing God in the face of suffering and disappointment. David's blessing is not an outburst of emotion, but an act of faithfulness.

As David writes this psalm, he is long past the strength of his youth. He has seen his life flourish and fade, and he senses the ultimate impermanence of all his efforts and accomplishments. He has seen many good things in his life but has had countless heartaches as well. The most bitter thought for him is that he has not always been faithful; he has disobeyed God, and greatly. There is no appeal here, as in earlier psalms, to David's integrity.[8] There is, instead, a long discourse on the gentleness and forbearance with which God disciplines his children.

David has benefited from that gentleness and forbearance, but it must have been a great disappointment for him that he needed to have those benefits applied to his own life. He has not lived up to God's standards or his own. It's a subdued David, then, who reflects on God's patience and steadfastness. And though he knows his own weakness, David is now determined to be what he has not always been in the past—faithful. And his faithfulness will begin with blessing the Lord.

In order to understand David's psalm, we need to be sure we understand what it means to bless the Lord. Blessing the

---

8. "The emphatic assertion of his innocence is gone for ever. Pardoned indeed he is, cleansed, conscious of God's favour, and able to rejoice in it; but carrying to the end the remembrance of his sore fall, and feeling it all the more penitently, the more he is sure of God's forgiveness." Alexander Maclaren, *Life of David: As Reflected in His Psalms* (Grand Rapids: Baker Book House, 1955), 258.

Lord is not a complicated concept, but it covers a perhaps surprising range of attitudes and actions.

The most common way to bless the Lord is by praising Him. Unfortunately, "Praise God!" has suffered from a long association with organized religion. It's one of those phrases (like "bless the Lord") that we tend to use mostly in church, and then without thinking too carefully about what we're saying. In order for the word *praise* to take on fresh meaning, we need to do two things: get the word out of the church, and get the church out of the word.

This shouldn't be hard since we often use the word *praise* outside of a religious context. I can praise my children, for example, either by bragging about them to others or by taking notice of something they've done and telling them, "Good job!" This comes to me fairly naturally. I'm proud of my children; it's easy for me to talk about their accomplishments or let them know when they've done well. It's possible—and maybe most meaningful—to praise God the same way. I suspect, in fact, that if I could learn to talk naturally and openly to my friends about God's character and specific things He does for me each day—to praise Him without saying "Praise God!"—it would have a far greater impact on them than my attempts to broach the subjects of eternal life or the reliability of the Bible.

A natural result of paying attention to the things that God does for us each day is to respond with thanks for those things. This, too, is an aspect of blessing God, and one that we tend to put a religious face on. "Saying the blessing" before a meal or "blessing the food" sounds somehow more reverent or significant than thanking God for it, but that's essentially what it means.[9]

---

9. Mark 8:6–7; see also 1 Corinthians 10:16. It could also be argued that when we "bless the bread," we sanctify it—we set it apart for God's use. In this way, too, we bless God by acknowledging His holiness and acting accordingly. "In your hearts set

Another way we use the word *bless* outside of church (if only barely outside it) is to say "God bless you" or simply "Bless you," as a way to wish someone well. At first it appears that this meaning of the word *bless,* at least, will not apply to blessing the Lord—because it simply wouldn't make sense to wish God's blessings upon God. Interestingly, though, it is in fact possible to bless God by expressing a desire that things go well for Him, that His purposes would be fulfilled.

This is an odd-sounding idea. Why would it make any difference whatsoever to express a hope that things go well for God? If God is God, if He is sovereign, His plans will be fulfilled whether we wish it or not. Yet many of us have blessed God in this way countless times, possibly without thinking about it, as we recite the Lord's Prayer: "Your kingdom come, your will be done on earth as it is in heaven."

Does expressing a desire that God's will be done make it any more likely that it will be done? Perhaps not, although it may remind us to try to live our own lives according to His will. But by expressing that desire, we identify ourselves with God; we commit ourselves to being on His side. We align ourselves with Him.

The idea of aligning ourselves with God is probably the best way to sum up all of what it means to bless Him. By acknowledging God, thanking and obeying Him, and expressing a desire that His plans be fulfilled, we align ourselves with God and His purposes.

David takes this idea of alignment with God a step further at the conclusion of Psalm 103, when he urges the angels and creation to bless God. They are, of course, already blessing Him—the angels through their obedience and creation

---

apart Christ as Lord," commands 1 Peter 3:15 (NIV)—sanctify Him, make him holy. Christ is already holy, of course, but when we sanctify Him in our hearts, we make Him holy to us; we bless Him.

through its silent witness to His power. But by expressing a desire that they bless God, David is saying that he wants to join in that blessing. "Your kingdom come," David prays, "your will be done *in me*, as it is in heaven."

⌀

It is in times of suffering, of course, that aligning yourself with God presents a special challenge. How can you align yourself with God's purposes when you don't understand what's happening around you? When your world has caved in on you?

But perhaps it's in such times that aligning yourself with God becomes truly meaningful.

The author of the book of Hebrews talks about offering to God "a sacrifice of praise."[10] The sacrifice of praise must cost us something. Every sacrifice has a price; that's what makes it a sacrifice. A sacrifice that doesn't cost anything is not worth anything.[11]

So perhaps praise that costs nothing is not worth much either—or, at least, not worth *as* much. It's easy to praise God when things are going well, and it's the right thing to do. But if we can offer praise to God only when we are basking in His blessings, it's an empty exercise. By praising God in the hard times—not by pretending to be happy, but by praising Him in the midst of sadness—we validate our praise for Him in the good times.

The more it costs us to praise Him, the more our praise is worth.

---

10. Hebrews 13:15
11. King David understood this well. See the story of his sacrifice in 2 Samuel 24, especially verses 22–24: "Then Araunah said to David, 'Let my lord the king take and offer up what seems good to him; here are the oxen for the burnt offering, and the threshing sledges and the yokes of the oxen for the wood. All this, O king, Araunah gives to the king . . .' But the king said to Araunah, 'No, but I will buy them from you for a price; I will not offer burnt offerings to the Lord my God that cost me nothing.' So David bought the threshing floor and the oxen for fifty shekels of silver."

David will bless God, regardless of what it costs him. His attitude seems to be, "Though my heart is heavy, I *will* bless the Lord. I know He loves me, no matter what happens, so I choose to bless Him. I'm on His side."

In his determination to stick with God despite his pain, David greatly resembles the most steadfast of the Old Testament sufferers, Job. "The Lord gives and the Lord takes away," Job said on the day that he lost his children, his wealth, and his reputation. "Blessed be the name of the Lord."

Sometimes people of faith have a hard time remembering that suffering was an excruciatingly painful process for Job. "The Lord gives and the Lord takes away; blessed be the name of the Lord," we quote Job brightly—forgetting that when he said it he had shaved his head and torn his clothes and that a few days later he was sitting on an ash heap, covered in painful boils and cursing the day he was born.

Job, while blessing the Lord, felt no compulsion to act the way a righteous man was expected to act. He questioned the justice of God, he begged God to leave him alone, he scrounged for answers to his dilemma in places that the theologians of his day thought inappropriate. He was, in fact, blessing God with everything in his being, by seeking out God honestly. "Yes, I will bless the Lord despite my suffering. I will bless Him with my very doubts and fears and despair, if I have to. I'll keep at Him with all that is within me until He responds. Though He slay me, yet will I trust him; I'll bless him if it kills me."[12]

⌒

I want to bless God like David, and like Job. Their responses tell me that I don't have to accept Allison's death blindly. I'm

---

12. Job 13:15 NKJV: "Though He slay me, yet will I trust Him. Even so, I will defend my own ways before Him."

allowed to question God; I'm allowed to be disappointed, even angry. I don't have to rest on religious platitudes, and I don't have to pretend that everything is okay. I don't have to rid myself of sadness before I can bless God.

If it's true that praise that costs more is worth more, then I have an opportunity now to offer praise that is more valuable than any I ever offered before. And it's with some surprise that I begin to find that I am capable of that kind of praise.

The day I first realized this I was out jogging. To be more accurate, perhaps I should say I was out shuffling. I quit exercising for a time after Allison's death, and when I finally got back to it my running didn't much resemble the running I had done before. Though I had never been the fastest runner, I was motivated; I would push myself to keep up a good pace, especially up hills. Now, not only was I out of shape, but my drive was gone too. I was likely to get halfway up a hill and think, "What possible difference does it make if I run up this hill? What matters at all?" And then I would stop and walk.

I did a lot of stopping and walking on my runs, and some crying as well. And, since I ran on farm roads that I had pretty much to myself, I even engaged in some yelling a time or two. I got into the habit of talking aloud with God—kind of like praying, only with the church taken out.

One rainy day as I was walking and questioning and feeling like the end of the world, I looked up across the valley to the far side of Pamplona. There was a dark cloud over the hill there, but a bright ray of sun was blasting out from behind the cloud, illuminating the brilliant green of the grass on the side of the hill below and the bright white of the sheep grazing on it. The contrast of this bright hill surrounded by the dark, dreary landscape around it was breathtaking; it was like a diamond set in brick.

"Good job, Lord," I said aloud.

This, I hope, is the sacrifice of praise—a simple acknowledgment of God's blessings on a backdrop of pain. This is the kind of praise I want to cultivate in my life; this is the kind of blessing for which I want to be known. It is praise that doesn't refuse to question but that rises out of the questioning and transcends it.

> Though the fig tree does not blossom,
>   and no fruit is on the vines;
> though the produce of the olive fails
>   and the fields yield no food;
> though the flock is cut off from the fold
>   and there is no herd in the stalls,
> yet I will rejoice in the Lord;
>   I will exult in the God of my salvation.[13]

I'm not sure I can exult yet. But I've found that even in the midst of suffering, I can be thankful for real blessings, even the small ones. From the depth of a pit, where I can see nothing around me and my way is walled up on all sides, I can still praise God for the star I see in the sky above me.

---

13. Habakkuk 3:17–18

CHAPTER 3

DO NOT FORGET:
THE STONE OF HELP

AS WE SORTED THROUGH THE THINGS IN ALLISON'S room in the days following her death, we found little worth keeping. Most of her treasures were those typical of thirteen-year-old girls—pictures of horses cut out of magazines, worn stuffed animals, tangles of string and cloth scraps from forgotten projects. Trinkets. Junk.

We're left with few physical reminders of her presence. She had drawn a picture of a horse; we have it framed and hung on the wall. At camp that summer she had made a little pillow out of a piece of truly hideous purple and green felt material. Sometime in the first week after her death, nine-year-old Nick brought it to our bedroom, jammed it between the headboard of our bed and the wall, and said, "Here, Mom—this is so you can remember Allison and don't have to feel bad anymore." We thanked him and hugged him and laughed when he left the room.

It's still there.

I wish I had more reminders of Allison. I don't want to forget anything about her. I wish I had a recording of her voice—a long conversation, not just snatches on a video from ten years ago. I go through periods when it becomes very important to me to create memorials of her: a photo album, a video, a keychain with her picture on it. So far, I've stopped short of following through on most of these plans. I didn't get a keychain; I have not yet made the video. I'm determined to remember Allison, but I want to do it right. I've found a constant, precarious tension there.

We have many beautiful pictures of Allison, most of them featuring her bright trademark smile. I'd like to hang these pictures on the walls, but I'm not sure I dare.

I don't want to increase attention to Allison at the cost of attention to our other children.

I want to share Allison's life with others, but I don't want to turn our living room into a shrine.

I'm afraid that pictures of Allison would dampen conversation; I'm afraid they will take the conversation in directions that some days, or with some visitors, I'd rather not go. I want to share Allison's memory with others; I want to guard it deep within myself.

I'd like to see those pictures every day, but I hate the thought that constant exposure to them would diminish their impact. I dread the day I walk past them without seeing them.

I like the idea of having a keychain with Alli's picture on it; I hate it, too. I want to keep her picture always at hand, but I don't want her memory turned into a good luck charm, a trinket. I don't want it reduced to keychains and videos and pictures on the wall. I don't want to cheapen her memory by making junk out of it.

❧

I will make something out of it, though. I understand, as I never did before, the importance of physical reminders, of memorials.

Years ago I stood in a church sanctuary, reading the plaques beneath each of the stained glass windows: "This window donated to the church in honor of . . ." *Why would you do that?* I remember thinking. *Surely everything done in this building should honor God. What would motivate you to insert someone else's name there?*

I know the answer to that question now. I find, as I try to put it into words, that it's not an uncomplicated answer. And I find as well that it goes beyond mere motivation. I'm not motivated to honor Allison's life; I'm compelled to honor it.

The compulsion comes from an intense desire to remember—or, rather, to *not forget*, which for some indefinable reason seems to me to be more fitting. We are determined not to forget Allison. Nor do we wish for others to forget her; she was priceless, irreplaceable. Everything that we do to honor her memory says, first of all, *"Do not forget Allison."*

If it didn't go further than that, though, a memorial would be superfluous; it would be impossible for us to forget Allison in any case. Our compulsion is not just to remember Allison but to remember the vow we made after her death: "I will never forget her; I will become a better person because of her influence on my life." This vow determines to make something good from evil, something meaningful from that which must not be allowed to be meaningless; it determines to create beauty from chaos. A stained glass window seems to me now a perfectly fitting tribute. So, too, does the gazebo that stands in a community park in a little town in Texas, built by a friend of mine and his brother in memory of their sister.

A few months ago I finished work on a similar, if simpler, memorial. With the help of friends, I built a carpetball table at the camp at which Allison worked during her last summer with us. (Carpetball is a simple game loosely related to bowling.) These friends might be surprised to find that the table was built in honor of Allison; you won't find her name on it, and, until now, I told no one my full reasons for building it. I found the physical labor involved to have a healing quality. With every board placed and painted, I thought of Allison; every blow of the hammer and every stroke of the brush offered my emotions the relief of a physical outlet; every minute spent working with new friends or strengthening old friendships reminded me of my desire to appreciate others as Allison did.

I found, too, that physical labor can itself become an important element of the memorial. The sacrifice of time and effort is in part a fulfillment of the vow to become a better person and in part a promise to continue to pursue that goal. Creating the memorial can be almost a sacred enterprise, holy, set apart—a vow to remember the things in life that are truly important. The point of the stained glass window is not ultimately its beauty, but rather its power to remind us continually of our desire to make the world a more beautiful place.

If a memorial were not a promise, it could only be a disappointment. Because we find that the tribute never sufficiently honors its subject, and we see that what is sacred to us means little to others: the window is broken by a baseball; the gazebo gets covered by graffiti. When that happens, the only thing that can keep it from feeling like another great loss is remembering that the memorial is not an end in itself but a promise, a vow, a reminder.

With my description of a memorial as a sacred work, I suppose I'm back on shaky theological ground: the appearance of giving the honor to someone else that should go to God. I don't think, though, that the one need replace the other. My vow to remember Allison is contained in my vow to remember God. Allison's death prompted me to promise to become a better person; God's blessings remind me that a good person is one who honors and follows Him.

I'm not sure if this explanation would have persuaded the young man who stood in front of those stained glass windows a lifetime ago. I don't say he was wrong. But I myself have come to see the argument for memorials as quite compelling.

The people of Israel were big on physical reminders, especially reminders of their encounters with God. They were forever building altars or piling up rocks and naming them. Jacob took a stone he had used as a pillow, set it up as a pillar, and called it Bethel (House of God); Moses built an altar and named it The Lord is my Banner following a victory over the Amalekites.[14]

Samuel, the prophet who judged Israel before he anointed Saul (and later, David) as king, set up his own monument after leading the people of Israel to a great and unlikely victory over the Philistines. "Then Samuel took a stone and set it up between Mizpah and Jeshanah, and named it Ebenezer [Stone of Help]; for he said, 'Thus far the Lord has helped us.'"[15]

Samuel didn't want the people ever to forget that victory, so he set it in stone. He was saying, "When things look bad, when you're tempted not to trust God, to doubt His love for you, look at the rock and remember: God has helped us this far. If He did this for us in the past, He did it because He loved us. And He won't give up on us now." The clear implication of "Thus far [He] has helped us" is, "We can trust him to help us the rest of the way."

I like to think of Psalm 103:2–5 as David's Ebenezer:

Bless the Lord, O my soul,
    and do not forget all his benefits—
who forgives all your iniquity,
    who heals all your diseases,
who redeems your life from the Pit,
    who crowns you with steadfast love and mercy,
who satisfies you with good as long as you live
    so that your youth is renewed like the eagle's.

---

14. Genesis 28:19; Exodus 17:15
15. 1 Samuel 7:12

David reminds himself here of some of the ways that God has demonstrated His love. Perhaps, as some have assumed, David wrote this psalm during a time of blessing from God, in response to answered prayer. But it seems more likely that David wrote it at a time of great personal struggle and emotional turmoil: "Does God really care for me? How do I know?" And so he answers himself: "I know God loves me because He has given me countless indications of His love. He's done all these things for me in the past, so I can trust Him to take care of me in the future."

In either case, the result is the same: a written reminder that David can turn to in tough times when God seems distant—a stone of help. "The Lord has helped me this far."

David's list of blessings is split neatly between bad things from which the Lord has delivered him—iniquity, diseases, destruction—and good things the Lord has heaped on him over and above his bare necessities: a crown of love and mercy, satisfaction with life, renewed youth.

I like the image of the crown. There's something captivating about the idea of the Lord of all creation, the great King himself, placing on our heads a crown of love and mercy. It's the extra, unexpected blessing, the icing on the cake. After He meets our basic needs, He showers us with more than we ever would have—or could have—thought to ask for.

The apostle Paul would take up this thought some ten centuries later: God, he says, is working within us "to accomplish abundantly far more than all we can ask or imagine."[16] God has a plan to give us undeserved, unimaginable, unlimited blessings.

I'm ready for them.

---

16. Ephesians 3:20

I'm ready to be crowned and satisfied; I could use some of that renewed youth. People used to comment on how young I looked. And I felt young. A couple of years ago, there was the heart of a twenty-two-year-old in my forty-five-year-old body. Now, I feel like I'm about seventy.

It's easy for me to agree with Paul when he says we can't imagine what God has in store for us. It's hard for me to see the destination God has in mind; some days, it's hard to believe that destination is out there. Like David, though, I can remind myself that I have seen evidence of God's faithfulness, milestones along the way He is leading us. Our family has tried to make a habit of noticing those milestones. Here are three of them, all from our time in Romania.

Living conditions improved dramatically over the ten years we lived in Romania. When we finally left Romania in 2004, we were spending much less time on basic survival activities like hunting down food. In the early years, though, being in Romania with a family full of young children offered significant challenges.

One day, we had no milk. There was none available anywhere in the stores, anywhere in the city. I was off on some errand when Jodi gathered all the kids together and prayed with them. "Lord, we know that you know our need. It's not an emergency—you know we can survive without milk. But please, Lord, send us milk today." A little while later there was a knock on the door. It was Sandu, the brother of our friend Ion, with four liters of milk. Sandu was sixty-eight years old but in bad health; he looked eighty. He had ridden his bike (and walked it, up the quarter-mile hill leading to our apartment building) three miles from his house to ours. He had never brought us milk or visited us before, and he never did it again. But that day, when we needed milk, he came.

God crowns us with love and mercy; He satisfies us with good.

The icing on the cake that day was milk.

⌒

Being crowned with steadfast love and mercy is a joy; having your life redeemed from the pit is almost inexpressible.

Though I've been reading the Bible for most of my life, there are only three occasions when it seemed to address me personally, as if the words I was reading were written especially for the circumstances I was living as I read them. The third of these occasions was as I read Psalm 103 in the weeks after Allison's death; the second was the birth of Andrea. The first was in September 1999, when my son Nate broke his back while we were living in Romania. Here's how I described the event in a letter to friends.

Sun., Sept. 19, 7:40 p.m.

Anna and Nate are late returning from a picnic with our teenage and college-age friends; I'll have to go look for them. "Somebody better be hurt," I say to myself, "or I'm going to be upset."

8:15 p.m. *My eight-year-old son Nate lies at my feet on a makeshift stretcher. His face is white, his breath shallow. Forty-five minutes ago a tree fell on his back.*

He can still move his fingers and toes, a good sign. But I'm concerned about internal injuries—someone saw him spit up a little blood right after the accident, and I see no cuts on his mouth or tongue.

As bad as things are now, the real danger is ahead of us—a trip to the hospital. We say a prayer together and carefully load Nate into the van.

> *The snares of death confronted me. In my distress*
> *I call upon the Lord; to my God I cried for help.*
> *Let your steadfast love, O Lord, be upon us, even*
> *as we hope in you.*

9:30 p.m. *The second we step into the emergency room, the attending physician begins to yell at us. Somewhere he has heard that good doctors are arrogant, and he considers himself a good doctor. "Get out of the room!" he yells at me, so I do, leaving Jodi with Nate. I return to our friends in the lobby with a thoughtful expression on my face. "I'm going to have to poke that guy in the eye before I leave," I tell them.*

Jodi agrees in principle if not method. "Somebody should pop that guy in the mouth," she fumes after the examination. The doctor has not only insulted and berated her during the entire examination—he has forced Nate to sit up to ascertain whether there's any spinal cord damage. If there is, he has undoubtedly made it worse.

During our twelve hours in this hospital we will get a very close look at what one of our disgusted Romanian friends calls "pure communism." The combination of incompetence, arrogance, and abuse of power makes me understand for the first time those who despair of any significant change for the better in Romania.

> *The face of the Lord is against evildoers, to cut off*
> *the remembrance of them from the earth. Make*
> *them bear their guilt, O God; let them fall by their*
> *own counsels. Let the wicked come to an end, but*
> *establish the righteous.*

Sun., Sept. 19, 11:30 p.m. *The hospital is quiet. They've agreed to let me sleep in the bed next to Nate. X-rays have* *shown that he has two compression fractures in his spinal column. The doctors see no evidence of internal bleeding, but I don't trust the doctors.*

Tomorrow we will drive Nate to Bucharest to get an MRI to check for spinal cord damage. But what if something happens during the night? "Lord, we put our trust in you. Please take care of us."

> *God is our refuge and strength, a very present help in trouble. I will both lie down and sleep in peace; for you alone, O Lord, make me lie down in safety. Under your wings I will find refuge; your faithfulness is my shield. I will not fear the terror of the night.*

Bucharest—Mon., Sept. 20 *On the way to Bucharest, I hear the details of the accident for the first time. As the group headed home, they passed a large log lying at the top of a steep slope. They decided—as young people will—to lift the log and watch it roll to the bottom. Several of them lifted it up, and then it slipped from their control, pinning Nate below it as it fell.*

The Romanian doctor at the hospital is extremely pleasant and helpful. The MRI confirms that there is no spinal cord damage or other internal injuries. Nate should rest in bed for two weeks before walking or standing and be confined to the apartment for another four, but he's going to be fine.

This may be the best day of my life.

> *I love you with my whole heart, O Lord, my strength! You are my rock, my fortress, my deliverer! I will praise the Lord with my whole heart,*

*I will tell of his wonders. You are my joy and my
happiness. I sing to the Lord, because he has been
good to me!*

Sun., Sept. 26 *More than fifty people come to a party
to celebrate God's protection of Nate. Many of them have
resisted coming to church, but tonight they share with us a
little of the joy of the Lord and the fellowship of believers.*

*I preached on Psalms this morning. I've read them hun-
dreds of times before, but for some reason I never really
understood them until this week.*

> *Come and see what God has done. Bless our God,
> O peoples, let the sound of his praise be heard, who
> has kept us among the living, and has not let our feet
> slip. Come and hear, all you who fear God, and I
> will tell what he has done for me. Truly God has lis-
> tened; he has given heed to the words of my prayer.*

*As a father has compassion for his children, so the Lord
has compassion for those who fear him (Psalm 103:13).*

Today, nearly nine years after Nate's accident, I can add a
few footnotes to that newsletter.

Nate is seventeen years old and doing well. Shortly after the
accident, an American doctor friend who examined Nate told
us that he would suffer some stiffness in his back during rainy
weather—when he's eighty years old! We can live with that.
So far, though, he shows no sign of slowing down. He ran on
the track team this year and recently competed in the Spanish
national championship in the 400 meter dash. He didn't win;
we can live with that, too.

Do not forget all his benefits . . . Yes, I've experienced the steadfast love of God.

I feel constrained to point out that many Romanians are doing the best they can to live with dignity amid trying conditions. Though poor, they are generous, thoughtful, encouraging. Others, unfortunately, like the doctor we ran into in the hospital, derive their sense of worth from treating others shabbily. This doctor, we found out later, was also insulted that we had stopped by a private clinic before we went to the hospital and that we had not offered him a bribe as soon as we came in the door.

Most notable about the letter, though, is the obvious way that the Psalms came alive with meaning for me. I had read those passages about danger, distress, and deliverance countless times before, but without having experienced a real time of distress, I wasn't able to appreciate them fully. Nate's accident was a good introduction to David's psalms. As a matter of fact, for truly understanding distress I think you'd be hard put to choose between living in caves while you flee for your life from King Saul and being subjected to the care of a rabid Romanian doctor. I know which I'd prefer.

Especially noteworthy is my quote of Psalm 103:13, which I would meet seven years later in far different circumstances.

◦━

My last story of God's care for us in Romania stars Allison.

Allison slept in a room with her sisters in a trundle bed that slid under a bunk bed during the day. Our apartment in Romania was cold, especially during the many years before we had central heating. We warmed the rooms at night with electric space heaters.

One night shortly after Jodi put the girls to bed, she was suddenly struck with a strange and unsettling fear: "What if I set the space heater too closely to Alli's bed? And what if Allison rolled over and her blanket fell over the heater, starting a fire? We could lose all the girls!" She hurried back to the room and found that Alli's blanket was indeed over the heater, and had already started to burn. She got to it just in time.

Allison used to tell this story to friends back in the United States. We saved the blanket, and she would show it to a Sunday school or church group as she told the story. We didn't name the blanket Ebenezer, but it wouldn't have been a bad idea.

⌒

We still have Allison's charred blanket. Today, though, rather than simply calling us to thankfulness, it also stirs up many questions. God took miraculous care of Allison; God let Allison die. How do we fit both of those events into our understanding of God's character?

Psalm 103 tells us that the gentleness of God is one of His hallmarks. He remembers that we are dust, and so He treats us with the utmost care. We see this, strangely, even in the circumstances of Allison's death. As terrible as it was for all of us, it could have been much worse, and though we don't understand why Allison had to die, we're grateful for the ways that God showed us, even on that awful day, that He was taking care of us.

We are grateful that Allison's last conscious moments were at home, while surrounded by her family. The week before, we had been at a conference where Allison had done a lot of running around and playing games and had even run an eight-kilometer race. Any of these activities might have triggered an incident. As hard as Allison's death was for us, it was so much better to have been with her than to have had someone from outside the family come to us with the news of her collapse.

We are grateful for that week she enjoyed with her friends. We're grateful, also, that she had a chance to be baptized at that conference. We're grateful that she knew God and was looking forward to meeting Him one day.

We're grateful that everyone in the family was on good terms with Allison when she died. There is no remorse over unresolved spats or harsh punishments or ugly words that we never had time to take back.

We're grateful that this didn't happen while we were in Romania, where the medical facilities and staff are at best limited, and often barbaric. The staff at the Pamplona hospital was gentle, professional, and considerate.

We're grateful that the circumstances of Allison's death made her an ideal organ donor. The doctors told us that six people's lives, at least, would be saved because of those donations. It's a good thing for all of them that I never had a chance to choose between them and Alli. But since she was gone, it was a blessing to us that her death should be of such significant benefit for others.

It was a blessing that there was a group of neighborhood children playing in the street outside our door when we carried Allison to the car to rush her to the hospital. We did not know our neighbors well; I wouldn't have wanted them to be uninformed of our tragedy, but neither could I have knocked on their doors and told them of it. The kids told their parents what they had seen; their parents came to us, and word traveled through the neighborhood.

We're grateful that we were thus able to meet or to get to know better many of the neighbors. We're grateful to them for their sympathy and thankful for those who took the time to come to the memorial service.

We're grateful that Allison did not experience a great deal of pain. We're grateful that she didn't suffer a debilitating brain injury that took away her personality and her spirit long before it took her body. We're grateful that she didn't die in any one of countless other more devastating circumstances.

These were all small but real blessings, and our thankfulness, though not unmixed with sorrow, is sincere.

Thus far has God helped us.

⌒

And so we see, even in our tragedy, evidence of God's love. But why? Why? If God loves us, why?

We live in a suburb of Pamplona, Spain, a city that's famous throughout the world for its annual festival, during which thousands of people—many fueled by alcohol—deliberately pack themselves tightly into narrow streets for the privilege of running for their lives from insanely huge, panicked bulls with razor-sharp horns. Most come through it without injury. There hasn't been a fatality in fifteen years.

My beautiful, happy daughter died while sitting in the living room helping her little sister eat lunch.

Three years ago, if I had been asked about the problem of the existence of suffering in a world created by a God supposedly both omnipotent and loving, I could have attempted an answer or two, but my ultimate conclusion would have been simply, "I don't know."

Today, my answer is still, "I don't know." But the "I don't know" has a different quality from the "I don't know" of three years ago. What I knew before, I knew in theory; now I know through experience. Today, my answer is, "I don't know. But God knows, and I can trust Him to sort it out in the end. I won't forget Allison, but neither will I let myself forget God's blessing. And I will bless Him, even when I can't make sense of His ways."

CHAPTER 4

FORGIVENESS: HEAVEN THAT STARTS ON EARTH

IT'S NOT UNUSUAL, I THINK, FOR PARENTS TO HAVE pet names for their children, and we're no different. When Allison was little, I called her my little black-hearted baby.

The fun in this nickname came mainly from shock value. Allison was a beautiful baby and toddler with a sweet disposition and a head full of blond curls. "Che papusha!" our Romanian friends used to say. "What a doll!" She was, too. So the incongruity of her nickname made for some great reactions. "Come here, you black-hearted baby!" I'd say, and Alli would smile and toddle over to me as the women in the room would gasp or shake their heads in disapproval. If I did this in the States, with my mother present, she would scold me. When she did so, I asked earnestly if there was something wrong with my theology: "Doesn't the Bible say that the heart is deceitful above all things and desperately wicked?" This thoroughly exasperated her, since she knew the theology was unassailable.

As hard as it is for me to remember it now, Allison was not perfect or perfectly innocent, not even as a baby. No kids are; they all come with a rebellious spirit as standard issue. Some of them disguise that rebellion better than others, but they've all got it. I've raised six kids, and I never had to teach a single one of them to whine, disobey, fight with his siblings, or generally misbehave. They all come up with that on their own. Allison was a good girl, but she needed forgiveness like anyone else. And it's a great comfort to me to know that she had it. One day when she was very young, she decided to live her life for Christ. She asked for forgiveness for her sin and received it.

The kind of hope Alli's forgiveness gives me is described by the apostle Paul: "But we do not want you to be uninformed, brothers and sisters, about those who have died, so that you may not grieve as others do who have no hope. For since we believe that Jesus died and rose again, even so, through Jesus, God will bring with him those who have died . . . Therefore encourage one another with these words."[17]

"Don't grieve without hope," Paul tells us. "Allison's life story did not end at her death."

Those words are indeed an encouragement; I don't know how I could go on without them, without the assurance that Allison is safe in God's hands. Allison believed in Jesus; her name was written in God's book; she put her faith in Him, and so now she is with Him.[18] This I believe; I've staked my life on it.

But I wish I could see it.

I wish, just for a second, that I could get a glimpse of Allison in the presence of God, glorifying and enjoying Him forever.

I wonder if she sees what's going on here, if she knows how much we miss her; if she knows how hard it is for us to be without her, how hard to believe that she's safer and happier than she's ever been before. I wonder how she would comfort and encourage us. If she were allowed to write us a letter, what could she say that would make it all better?

Maybe something like this:

---

17. 1 Thessalonians 4:13–14, 18
18. Philippians 4:3; Revelation 21:27

Dear Mom, Dad, Anna, Amber, Nate, Nick, and Andy,

Hi! I'll bet you didn't expect to hear from me. I didn't really expect to write to you, either, but I decided maybe you could use some encouragement. The other day Jesus gave me a hug and said, "That's from your family." I hugged Him back, tight, and told Him to pass it on to you. He said, "I have been." Have you felt it?

Heaven is great! It will be so good when we're all here together. There are a lot of things I'm looking forward to showing you. But even though I can't wait until you're here, and even though I love you all more than ever, I can't say that I miss you or even that I feel bad for you. There's just not room for that sort of feeling here. And the time on earth is so short, to me it's kind of like when you're just waiting for a good friend who's due to knock on the door in just a minute, and then you have a whole lifetime to do fun stuff together.

The last time we saw each other went so quick, but that will only make seeing you again that much better. By the way, I did hear Mom and Dad and Nate and Amber telling me goodbye in the hospital room. I was telling you goodbye, too, even though you couldn't hear me—and telling Nick and Anna and Andrea goodbye, too.

I'm sorry you're going through such a hard time, but it won't last forever. When you get here, we'll be enjoying ourselves too much to think about it. I asked Jesus if I could write and tell you all about heaven, and He smiled and said, "Sure, tell them whatever you like." I thought at first He was going to laugh, and I didn't know why. And then after thinking and thinking about what to say, I realized that there isn't any way to tell you about what heaven's like in a way that you could really understand. Not to rub it in, but the way you look at things—or maybe I could say your intelligence—is still pretty limited right now.

So I asked Him how I could do it. He said, "I'll give you the same advice I gave to Isaiah and John when they were going to write about heaven: use images they can understand, that are most like the real things you want to tell them about here." So here goes:

Heaven is like a big mansion with a lot of rooms in it. Everybody gets a room. Dad's stinks like fish, mine like horses. Nick's is filled right now with lots of stuff like Legos and family games. In Amber's room there are a bunch of people standing around, waiting for somebody to tell them what to do. (Just kidding, Amber!) And even though everybody has their own room, we're rarely alone, because we always like to enjoy the rooms together. When we walk into Dad's room, all of a sudden we have a terrific desire to fish. Everybody loves horses in my room. And when we open the door to Amber's room, we all look at her and—well, you know. And Jesus is in every room with us, all the time, and that's what really makes it heaven.

And almost none of this is close to what the truth actually is, but it's the best way I know to tell you this: heaven is good, and it's worth the wait. And everything you go through on earth is way worth having Jesus tell you "Well done!" when you get here.

Pass around lots of hugs for me. Be sure to give Dad one—he needs it. I love you! I'll see you soon! I know, because Jesus showed me all your names in the book!

Love,
Alli

I wrote that letter not too long after Allison's death. I told the kids one morning at breakfast that we had gotten a letter from Allison, and had Amber read it aloud. They liked it. We gave each other hugs all around. Jodi asked Nick what he thought.

"Hmm," he smiled. "Legos and family games. Cool!"

We didn't realize until the next day that nine-year-old Nick thought that the letter actually was from Allison. I guess I felt a little bad for him when his brother set him straight, but not much. He knows Alli is alive and enjoying herself in heaven; he knows he'll see her someday. He doesn't have to talk himself into it or quiet any doubts. His faith is the faith of a child, without which none of us can enter into the kingdom of heaven.

I believe; he knows. I hope he keeps that certainty for a long, long time.

⸺

Theology teaches us that to delight in God's presence—as I believe Allison is doing now—is not just a heavenly reality but also an earthly goal. "What is the chief end of man?" asks the Westminster Catechism, and offers the answer, "Man's chief end is to glorify God and to enjoy Him forever."

So theologically speaking, it makes good sense that David's list of blessings begins with forgiveness: "Do not forget all his benefits—who forgives all your iniquity. . ." Without forgiveness, we remain alienated from God, and we can neither glorify nor enjoy Him. Without forgiveness, we couldn't truly enjoy health or family or any other good thing. Forgiveness is the most important of God's blessings, the open door that leads to the enjoyment of all others. This is, in fact, the theme of the whole Bible: it is the story of God's forgiveness, the account of the incredible lengths to which God will go in order to restore fellowship with those who have rebelled against Him.

Theologically, too, the dispelling of sin is of the utmost practical importance to man because, according to the Bible, sin is the cause of all suffering in the world. Before Adam sinned, there was no suffering; now, the whole world suffers.

But speaking theologically is not David's aim here. He isn't writing to convict anyone of his sin. To those who do not see sin in their own lives or who do not view sin as a problem, David offers not a word. It is David's sin—not anyone else's—that concerns him; he's not writing about anyone's need for forgiveness but his own. And that need he knows all too well.

The problem of sin was heavy on David's mind as he wrote this psalm; that's why forgiveness of sin plays such a large part in it. Verses 7–14 abound in grateful praise of God not just for His constant patience and love but specifically for His patience and love demonstrated in the face of man's unfaithfulness. God pours out His mercy, grace, love, patience, and leniency on those who disobey. He is the God who gently brings us back into His good favor.

Verses 7 and 8 tell us much about David's state of mind as he composed the psalm:

> He made known his ways to Moses,
>   his acts to the people of Israel.
> The Lord is merciful and gracious,
>   slow to anger and abounding in steadfast love.
> He will not always accuse,
>   nor will he keep his anger forever.

The thoughts David expresses here are not original; he is quoting a passage from Exodus. The setting of this passage is the desert. God has sent Moses to deliver His people from Egypt and take them to the land He has promised. Along the way, though, they sin so grievously that God is ready to destroy them all. Moses begs God to forgive them and asks of Him, "Show me your ways." God relents (as David notes in Psalm 103:7, "He showed his ways to Moses") and reveals to Moses His ways, His character: "The Lord passed before him, and proclaimed,

> "The Lord, the Lord,
> a God merciful and gracious,
> slow to anger,
> and abounding in steadfast love and
>   faithfulness,
> keeping steadfast love for the thousandth
>   generation,
> forgiving iniquity and transgression and sin,
> yet by no means clearing the guilty . . ."[19]

Moses remembers this revelation; he clings to it. And shortly after, he reminds God of it when God—for good reason—is again ready to punish His people.

This time when Moses intercedes, he has a powerful weapon of persuasion—the Lord's own words: "Let the power of the Lord be great in the way that you promised when you spoke, saying,

> "The Lord is slow to anger,
> and abounding in steadfast love,
> forgiving iniquity and transgression . . ."

Forgive the iniquity of this people according to the greatness of your steadfast love, just as you have pardoned this people, from Egypt even until now."[20]

And God does forgive them—because He is a God slow to anger and abounding in steadfast love, and because He keeps His promises.

---

19. Exodus 34:6–7
20. Numbers 14:17–18, 19

The citing of this passage becomes a refrain in Israel. When the people have disobeyed God, when they've turned from God and have suffered God's punishment in return, they fall back on this passage in repentance, in desperation, and in hope.

If you have to quote this passage, it's because you've blown it. You've done wrong, rebelled against God, and there are no extenuating circumstances that would excuse your conduct. You have no other recourse than to fall before Him and repent—and to remind Him that He is a merciful God and will forgive. The prophet Joel cites this passage when the nation of Israel is being punished for its faithlessness. Nehemiah quotes it many centuries later, as the exiles stumble back from Babylon to Jerusalem.[21]

And David quotes it in Psalm 103.

So when David opens his list of God's blessings with forgiveness, he's not speaking as David, the theologian, but as David, the sinner.

David is a man who knew what it meant to suffer. In many situations, he suffered as an innocent man, a victim of the treachery and pettiness of others; but he also suffered at times because of his own sin, weaknesses, and poor choices. And he found, as we still do today, that the latter is a much heavier burden than the former. Because as frustrating as it is to be persecuted for doing what is right, there is in that case the consolation of knowing that God is on your side and will one day vindicate you. When we suffer because of our own actions, though, that consolation is taken from us. Our worst sorrows are those we bring on ourselves.

---

21. Joel 2:12–13; Nehemiah 9:17

David had to live with the bitter knowledge that he brought his suffering upon himself, and worse, that his sin caused the suffering of countless others. Perhaps worst of all, his sin separated him from fellowship with God. David was a man after God's heart.[22] He considered God his friend; he loved God. But he also sinned. When David sinned, his fellowship with God was broken; and when his fellowship with God was broken, so was his heart.

And so forgiveness of that sin—gentle, loving, total forgiveness and restoration of his relationship with God—was an unmerited blessing of unbelievable proportions.

◦——

As deeply as David felt the effects of forgiveness, he didn't know the whole story. Very little of what is in our Bible was available to him. He was not totally ignorant of God's plan to reconcile the world to himself—David prophesied about the coming of Jesus Christ nine hundred years or so before the event—but he did not have the privilege of seeing how God's plan unfolded, as we do. He did not see how God would defeat death, once and for all.

The good news of the Bible is that God has already defeated the power of sin through the death and resurrection of His Son, Jesus Christ. His forgiveness is available to all who believe. Christ's work is a great victory against sin, pain, and suffering. One day, He will deliver us not only from the punishment of sin, but also from its presence. We will suffer no more.

But while we're on this earth, we do suffer. And though God knows that the happy ending is coming, and knows how He will bring it about and how He will wipe away all tears forever, He is not untouched by our suffering. He is a God

---

22. 1 Samuel 13:14; Acts 13:22

who grieves, who takes note of our pain, who keeps our tears in a bottle. "Precious in the sight of the Lord is the death of his saints."[23]

But don't be uninformed. We do not grieve as do others, and neither does God. The death of those He loves is not without hope.

---

23. John 11:32–36; Psalm 56:8; Psalm 116:15 NIV

CHAPTER 5

WHEN GOD DOESN'T HEAL: ALL SHALL BE WELL

ONCE, WHEN (JESUS) WAS IN ONE OF THE CITIES, there was a man covered with leprosy. When he saw Jesus, he bowed with his face to the ground and begged him, 'Lord, if you choose, you can make me clean.' Then Jesus stretched out his hand, touched him, and said, 'I do choose. Be made clean.' Immediately the leprosy left him."[24]

> Bless the Lord, O my soul,
>> and do not forget all his benefits—
> who forgives all your iniquity,
>> who heals all your diseases . . .

"Who heals all your diseases"—except, of course, when He doesn't.

Sometimes—often—even the innocent suffer. Children suffer from a countless array of causes: congenital birth defects, deadly diseases, natural disaster. Where is the God who heals all our diseases when a child fights desperately against the cancer that will ultimately take his life?

"God, if you choose, you can heal my child."

"Yes, I can. But, well, not this time."

---

24. Luke 5:12–13

I'm thinking especially today of our friends Kevin and Kay Ann and their son Timothy. Timothy was diagnosed with cancer when he was eight years old. And so he underwent the pain and nausea and discomfort of treatment, until the cancer was gone.

And then it came back. He underwent treatment again. He did so with a bright spirit, a brave heart, and an amazing sense of humor.

And again the cancer came back. Three times over a five-year period, Timothy and his parents and his siblings were crushed by the news of this enemy's return. Finally, not long after Allison went to be with the Lord, Timothy joined her there.

Bless the Lord, who heals all your diseases.

Was David wrong? Fortunate in always being healed himself, did he falsely conclude that God always heals the diseases of those who love Him? Or having seen unhealed disease, did he forget or willfully ignore it?

No. David knows from hard experience that the innocent suffer along with the guilty, that health is never guaranteed, even for those who love God. Derek Kidner points out David's firsthand knowledge of this truth, citing the sad circumstances surrounding the death of David and Bathsheba's child: "For all the similarity of these two phrases, there is a difference between God's handling of *iniquity* and of *diseases*, which was made plain in David's own case when he repented of his sin . . . Forgiveness was immediate; but healing was denied, in spite of seven days of prayer and fasting (2 Sa. 12:13–23)."[25]

Sometimes healing is denied; sometimes we suffer. Health is a great blessing from God, but it is not a promise. Healing, like so many of God's blessings, is never guaranteed, as Mark

---

25. *Psalms 73-150* (Downers Grove, IL: InterVarsity Press, 1978), 364–365.

Buchanan points out: "His faithfulness is made known in countless things—sun and rain, food and air, shelter and freedom, health and safety. But God never guarantees these things. They are expressions of His faithfulness, but not its essence."[26] Sometimes we don't see God's favor through physical blessings. Sometimes we suffer. This fact leads to at least two important questions: *Why?* and *How will I respond?*

Psalm 103 answers the second of these questions. David's response is to call himself to bless God, to remind himself of the many things God has done for him, of the times that God *has* healed. Because each of those healings is an indication of God's love, evidence that He can be trusted even when He does not heal.

The other question—the why—is not directly addressed in Psalm 103. Why does God not always give immediate healing, as He offers immediate forgiveness? David doesn't venture a guess. But Kidner notes, "If relationship with God is paramount, this makes good sense, for sin destroys it, while suffering may deepen it (Heb. 5:8; 12:11)."[27]

In this statement we have the *beginning* of a *hint* of a *possible* reason for suffering—that God allows suffering in part because it offers us the potential of strengthening our relationship with Him.

All in all, it's not a very satisfactory explanation. If it's true that a parent can learn about God and draw closer to Him through the death of a child—and I believe it is—many questions remain unanswered.

Was it really necessary for us to learn those things? It must not have been, since so many others aren't required to learn them.

Was it so important that Allison—or Timothy—had to die?

---

26. *The Holy Wild* (Sisters, OR: Multnomah Press, 2003), 69–70.
27. *Psalms*, 365.

Was it worth it?

I don't know; I don't have the answers to those questions. Something deep within me, I have to admit, recoils from even considering them. I would gladly have given my life for Allison. That I could benefit in any way from her death seems inappropriate, if not repellant.

And yet the idea that I would not be changed by Allison's death is worse. So it is some comfort to see that Kidner is right: Allison's death has pushed me closer to God. This is the silver lining on a very dark cloud. The cloud itself remains as black as ever, but the lining grows brighter and wider with each new insight I gain into God's character, with each reminder of His faithfulness.

⌒

I've gained new insight into God's faithfulness as a result of my daughter's death. It is a comfort to be pushed closer to a God who can heal all our diseases, but sometimes chooses not to.

If what I've just said makes perfect sense to you, perhaps you're not paying close enough attention.

It doesn't make sense to me. And yet, as I step back and ponder these sentences, I find that though they shouldn't make sense, I believe them. God lets terrible things happen; I can trust God implicitly.

Believing without understanding isn't really something new with me. It's an uncomfortable fact of my daily existence that certain things persist in being true even when I don't understand them. Things like electricity and internal combustion and microwaves and photosynthesis happen around me all the time, and as yet I don't really have a clue how. I'm like the man Mark Twain described whose ignorance covered the world like a blanket with hardly a hole in it anywhere.

I suppose, though, that everybody's belief must exceed his understanding. As sawdust-trail evangelist Billy Sunday tactfully put it, "If you only believe things that you can understand you must be an awful ignoramus."[28] But trying to sort out these thoughts on suffering has become important to me. Even knowing I'll never completely understand, I can't keep from trying.

So how can it be true that we can trust the God who heals all our diseases, even when He doesn't heal all our diseases? My own attempt to reconcile these truths begins with the premise that Allison's death was not the will of God.

Christianity is not a religion—there are some—in which "God's will" is synonymous with fate, meaning that if something happened, God wanted it to happen, and so the righteous response is to accept it without questioning. Many things happen that God did not want and of which He does not approve. This is evidenced, in part, by His wrath. The Bible portrays a God who is always in control but is not always pleased. Events or human actions cannot thwart Him, but they do sometimes anger Him. This is why we pray, "Your will be done on earth, as it is in heaven." Yes, we pray it in order to align our own hearts to His purposes, but we also pray it because, clearly, His will is *not* always done here on earth.[29]

I don't mean to imply that Allison's death was beyond God's foresight or control. I don't believe anything is outside

---

28. William T. Ellis, *Billy Sunday: The Man and His Message* (Philadelphia: John C. Winston Co., n.d.), 79.

29. One important example should suffice: It is not the will of God that anyone go to hell. "The Lord is not slow about his promise, as some think of slowness, but is patient with you, not wanting ["not willing that" NKJV] any to perish, but all to come to repentance" (2 Peter 3: 9). And yet it seems that many more will perish than otherwise. The road to heaven is narrow, the road to hell broad. All religions do not lead to God; God is patient, but He is also jealous. He insists that we worship only Him and that we worship Him in the way He prescribes. Jesus Christ is the way He has appointed, and He is the only way. "I am the way, and the truth, and the life," said Jesus. "No one comes to the Father except through me" (John 14:6). God will not prevent anyone by force from turning away from Him and toward their own destruction, but it gives Him no pleasure to see them do so.

God's control; He is neither surprised nor dismayed by the storms that come into our lives. He uses them, somehow, to turn them to our good. (We'll come back to that in a minute.) But God is not the creator of evil; He is not the author of Alli's death.

It may seem that I'm splitting hairs, sweeping the hard questions under a rug of semantics. In truth, the point I'm making doesn't answer them. If Allison's death was not His will, why did He not prevent it? If God is all-powerful, then why doesn't He do away with evil and death immediately? After all is said and done, doesn't God bear the responsibility for our pain? "If not he," as Job asked, "then who?"[30]

I think it helpful, though, to distinguish between what God allows and what He wants. If *God's will* is to have any useful definition—that is, any definition beyond *everything that happens*—it must be that which He desires, that which gives Him pleasure. There are lots of things in the world that do not fall into this category. It is not God's will, for example, that we sin. God did not plan or create sin. Hatred, gossip, greed, rape, murder—none of these are His will.

Neither is death. Death is not natural; it is not part of God's perfect plan for the world; it should not be borne with quiet fortitude. It should make us angry. Not at God, but at Satan and sin. This is true whether the death is that of a ninety-year-old man or a newborn. Death is not God's will.

That is why it is on its way out; that is why Christ has already won the victory over death and one day will destroy death forever.

ᗡ

So I do not believe that Allison's death was God's will.

---

30. Job 9:24

I do believe, however, that God is using Allison's death to bring good things to my life. He is transforming that terrible day, giving it meaning, as He transforms me. This does not mean that He planned Allison's death for the purpose of transforming me. It does give an indication, though, that His ultimate purpose is not deterred, derailed, or delayed by any circumstances. God can, and does, create something good out of everything in my life.

As the fourteenth-century mystic Julian of Norwich famously wrote, "All shall be well, and all shall be well, and all manner of things shall be well."

I said earlier that the items on the list of Psalm 103:3–5 are indications of God's love rather than promises. But there are promises and guarantees, many of them, in the Bible. Here's one from Romans 8:28: "All things work together for good for those who love God."

This promise has been held tightly by God's people through twenty centuries and countless trials. It's the promise that God has a plan—a good and even perfect plan—for each of those who love Him, and that no circumstances will interfere with that plan.

How could Allison's death lead to my good? Certainly, the good must consist of much more than the trivial pleasantness that we often associate with goodness. Swiss theologian Frederick Godet wrote, "It means not only any good result whatever in which everything issues for the believer, but that constant progress to the final goal to which the plan of God leads us, and which constitutes our real destination."[31]

Both our real destination and the path to it define the truly good. And God guarantees that everything in the lives of those who love Him—good, bad, painful, embarrassing,

---

31. F. Godet, *St. Paul's Epistle to the Romans*, vol. 2 (Edinburgh: T. & T. Clark, 1881), 105.

trivial—will contribute to our attainment of that destination. Somehow, against all our present understanding, it will become evident in eternity that nothing in life was as important as that journey to experiencing God's good in us.

It's hard for us to see that now. Various believers over the years have compared our earthly perspective to the view of the back side of an exquisite tapestry. On that side, all is confusion—a mess of twisted, tangled threads and ugly knots. On the other side, though, the tapestry is intricately beautiful, flawless. Ravi Zacharias writes, "His design for your life pulls together every thread of your existence into a magnificent work of art. Every thread matters and has a specific purpose."[32]

All things work together for good for those who love God.

This is the promise that makes suffering bearable. *God has a plan*, and the fulfillment of that plan will overrule anything that we have to go through to obtain it: "I consider that the sufferings of this present time are not worth comparing with the glory about to be revealed to us," wrote the apostle Paul.[33] One day, God will truly crown us, once and for all, with His steadfast love and mercy, and satisfy us with good.

> No eye has seen,
>> no ear has heard,
>> no mind has conceived,
>> what God has prepared for those who love
>> him.[34]

I believe that. I believe that God will use everything that happens to me to perform His purposes in my life. One day I'll see the front of the tapestry and not the back.

---

32. Ravi Zacharias, *The Grand Weaver* (Grand Rapids: Zondervan, 2007), 17.
33. Romans 8:18
34. 1 Corinthians 2:9 NIV

David believed it too. That's why he can write with confidence that God heals all diseases. In addition to past blessings, David has in mind the ultimate purposes of God. It's this assurance of the ultimate accomplishment of God's purposes, points out Alexander Maclaren, which allows David to thank God for deliverance when he is yet in the throes of distress. "Save me, O God, by your name, and vindicate me by your might," starts out Psalm 54, and moves quickly—even before his actual deliverance—to, "For he has delivered me from every trouble, and my eye has looked in triumph on my enemies" (v. 7). David's seemingly premature thankfulness "may assure us that whosoever seeks for the salvation of that mighty name may, even in the midst of trouble, rejoice as in an accomplished deliverance."[35] As David can thank God for complete deliverance from his enemies even while they still have the upper hand, even so can he thank God for his healing of *all* diseases in a world that is still subject to them.

Some days I hold this promise not only firmly, but easily. Other days my faith is not so strong, and the prospect of meeting God and Allison and laughing together with them seems faint and unlikely.

On those days, I grip that promise even more tightly.

---

35. Alexander Maclaren, *Life of David* (Grand Rapids: Baker Book House, 1955), 104.

DAVID'S FRIEND PAUL

DAVID AND THE APOSTLE PAUL DIDN'T ACTUALLY SPEND much time together here on earth, living as they did some thousand years apart. I think they'll have some interesting conversations, though, in the days of "eternal weight of glory beyond all measure."[36]

Here's a more complete text of the section from Romans 8 that I quoted in the last chapter. Like Psalm 103, it's a passage of hope amidst pain, of God's loving presence in life's dark hours, and of ultimate victory for those who trust in Him.

ROMANS 8:18–39

I consider that the sufferings of this present time are not worth comparing with the glory about to be revealed to us. For the creation waits with eager longing for the revealing of the children of God; for the creation was subjected to futility, not of its own will but by the will of the one who subjected it, in hope that the creation itself will be set free from its bondage to decay and will obtain the freedom of the glory of the children of God. We know that the whole creation has been groaning in labor pains until now; and not only the creation, but we ourselves, who have the first fruits of the Spirit, groan inwardly while we wait for adoption, the redemption of our bodies. For in hope we were saved. Now hope that is seen is not hope. For who hopes for what is seen? But

---

36. 2 Corinthians 4:17

if we hope for what we do not see, we wait for it with patience.

Likewise the Spirit helps us in our weakness; for we do not know how to pray as we ought, but that very Spirit intercedes with sighs too deep for words. And God, who searches the heart, knows what is the mind of the Spirit, because the Spirit intercedes for the saints according to the will of God.

We know that all things work together for good for those who love God, who are called according to his purpose. For those whom he foreknew he also predestined to be conformed to the image of his Son, in order that he might be the firstborn within a large family. And those whom he predestined he also called; and those whom he called he also justified; and those whom he justified he also glorified.

What then are we to say about these things? If God is for us, who is against us? He who did not withhold his own Son, but gave him up for all of us, will he not with him also give us everything else? Who will bring any charge against God's elect? It is God who justifies. Who is to condemn? It is Christ Jesus, who died, yes, who was raised, who is at the right hand of God, who indeed intercedes for us. Who will separate us from the love of Christ? Will hardship, or distress, or persecution, or famine, or nakedness, or peril, or sword? As it is written,

> "For your sake we are being killed all day long;
>   we are accounted as sheep to be
> slaughtered."

No, in all these things we are more than conquerors through him who loved us. For I am convinced that neither death, nor life, nor angels, nor rulers, nor things present, nor things to come, nor powers, nor height, nor depth, nor anything else in all creation, will be able to separate us from the love of God in Christ Jesus our Lord.

CHAPTER 6

A FATHER'S COMPASSION: DAVID'S PSALM

BY THE TIME I HAD READ PSALM 103 EVERY DAY FOR six months or so, I was starting to feel like it was my psalm. It spoke to my heart; it expressed my emotions; it lifted my discouragement and motivated me to bless God through my pain.

Yet I knew, too, that it wasn't my psalm; it was David's. And I knew that although personal experiences can aid us greatly in our understanding of what we read—because of Nate's accident and Allison's death I have much greater insight into expressions of joy and despair in the Psalms—they can also at times get in the way. We have a tendency to project onto the writers of Scripture, or even onto God, the emotions that we ourselves are experiencing. "Since he speaks so clearly to me in my circumstances, the author must have been undergoing similar circumstances," we reason, or even, "Since this particular interpretation of this passage gives me comfort in my suffering, it must be legitimate." I've tried to steer away from this tendency but would not be surprised to find that I have not always succeeded.

I knew, then, that the correct interpretation of Psalm 103 would be the meaning intended by its author, not a meaning I brought to it myself. I knew that in order to really understand what the passage meant to me, I would need to understand what it meant to David. And as I studied the psalm, I had to admit that there were parts of it that I did not understand very clearly.

I was especially puzzled by verse 6: "The Lord works vindication and justice for all who are oppressed."

Even after a lot of study and thought, I couldn't figure out what verse 6 was doing in Psalm 103. It seemed to me that structurally, thematically, artistically—you name it—it just did not belong. One verse about justice for the oppressed, and then, abruptly, without transition, eight verses about mercy for the guilty. That the verse was true I had no doubt; I just wasn't sure why it was included in this psalm. It stuck out; it seemed out of place. When I read the psalm without it, skipping from verse 5 to verse 7, I didn't miss it; the psalm seemed to flow better without it.

I knew, of course, that I was wrong; I knew that David put the verse there for a reason. I just couldn't see that reason for a long time.

And then one day, I suddenly found it. The solution that occurred to me came from an unexpected source—a description in the book of Ezra of the Jewish exiles returning to Jerusalem some five hundred years after David's time. Like the author of Psalm 103, these people were thankful for their deliverance from oppression, but also mindful that their suffering was caused by their own sin. The emotions engendered by their experience with these truths were profound, contradictory, and inextricably mixed. At the laying of the foundation of the new Temple,

> many of the priests and Levites and heads of families, old people who had seen the first house on its foundations, wept with a loud voice when they

saw this house, though many shouted aloud for
joy, so that the people could not distinguish the
sound of the joyful shout from the sound of the
people's weeping, for the people shouted so loudly
that the sound was heard far away.[37]

That's it! I realized. *If David wrote Psalm 103 at a time of heightened emotions, in a situation in which both the justice and the
mercy of God were apparent, it would be natural for him to move
quickly from the description of God's deliverance to one of God's
mercy.*

Perhaps David even intended to write more about God's
justice and then brought himself up short as he realized how
much greater the blessing of God's mercy had been for him.
His emotions may have been mixed, but not in equal parts:
they seem to have contained one part praise for God's justice
to about eight parts thanksgiving for His mercy. He's delivered,
yes; but above all, he's forgiven.

There were probably many situations in David's later life in
which both God's deliverance and His gentle hand of correc-
tion were evident. One that we know of, though, seems a particularly fitting setting for the writing of Psalm 103. There's no
reason why the psalm must have been written on that occasion,
of course; but if it were, it might have happened something like
this.

⌒

David stands alone before an open window in a large room
of a house in the city of Mahanaim, east of the Jordan River.
A breeze from the window sets the candle flickering and the
shadows dancing. David notices neither breeze nor candle as he

---

37. Ezra 3:12–13

looks out of the window toward the west, toward Jerusalem—Jerusalem, from which he fled in disgrace so recently. Now that the battle was over, would he return there again as king? It's not certain; tonight, he cannot bring himself to care.

From the square below him come the sounds of celebrating. The soldiers are reveling because that morning, when they went out to fight, they didn't know whether they would survive the day, and now they have not only survived it but emerged victorious. But they are celebrating not with abandon but with restraint because they love David—and David has lost a son.

David moves away from the window and sits down heavily. It seems to him that he is more tired at this moment than he has ever been in his life—more tired than in the days when he ran for his life from Saul in the wilderness, hungry and thirsty and afraid to rest; more tired than in the days of his youth when he lived and fought with his army. Today he fought no one—his generals refused to risk his life in battle—and so he stayed behind and waited, an old man waiting for word of his army and his son. It would have been far easier to fight; he is exhausted with waiting.

Still, he has no thought of sleep. He buries his face in his hands once again: "Absalom, my son, my son," he murmurs, but no tears come. He has cried much of the day and knows he will cry again, but now he feels empty of tears.

He feels empty of everything. He has passed through so many trials in the previous days—so much treachery, so much betrayal. Many friends have proven themselves loyal, too, but others have betrayed him . . . Mephibosheth, whose fortunes he had restored, who ate at his table. *I would have staked my life on the gratefulness and loyalty of Mephibosheth,* he thinks to himself.

And the ones who are with me—is the aid of Joab and Abishai worth the loss of a Mephibosheth? Joab and Abishai are fiercely loyal to David, but they are ruthless men, he knows, violent, vengeful, dangerous. And now Joab has shown a total lack of understanding for David's grief and has presumed a freedom to express himself to the king in a way that borders on insolence. *Perhaps it is time to replace Joab as head of the army.* But he will think of that no more tonight.

Without rising, David looks again toward the window and Jerusalem. He thinks about the old days, about friends and enemies long gone. Jonathan, his loyal best friend; King Saul, whom he would gladly have spent his life serving. He remembers again that from the city he is in, Mahanaim, Saul's son Ishbosheth ruled most of Israel for two years. *Weak and unwise, but unworthy of the treachery that killed him*, thinks David, *as was Ish-bosheth's captain Abner unworthy of the treachery that took his life. I did right to avenge Ish-bosheth's death. May God one day avenge Joab's treachery towards Abner.*

So many deaths; so many disappointments. *This is not the way I thought it would go all those years ago. This is not the way it should be.*

And yet most of his family is safe in Mahanaim with him. David's own life is safe. His army has triumphed. *These are not empty blessings*, David tells himself, *even though all you can see right now is the loss of Absalom.* And then, suddenly, he knows what he must do, though he doesn't want to—*because* he doesn't want to. He must bless his Lord. But can he? Can he once again worship through his tears?

David closes his eyes and begins to compose his psalm. *Bless the Lord, O my soul,* he orders himself. *And all that is within me, bless his holy name . . .*

⌒

And so David begins his psalm, knowing from the start that the "all that is within" him includes sorrow, weakness, sinfulness, unfaithfulness. Yet he knows too, whether instinc-tively or consciously, that his own weak character makes the strength, righteousness, and faithfulness of God that much more necessary and praiseworthy.

And so he blesses God, urging himself not to lose sight of the blessings he has enjoyed from God throughout his life. And there have been many of them.

There were the blessings he experienced as a shepherd boy so many years ago, before he was king or captain or warrior—when he was just young David, alone with the sheep and with God. There was the blessing of the Lord's quiet presence and the joy of composing and singing psalms of praise on his harp. There were also the blessings he enjoyed as he learned to trust God implicitly. "Take care of the sheep," his father told him, and certainly no boy ever took his father's orders more literally and faithfully. Jesse could not have imagined that David would fulfill that mandate above all reasonable expectations, going so far as to rescue sheep out of the mouths of bears and lions, chasing them down and killing them rather than running away in order to save himself and perhaps the rest of the flock. But it seemed a normal matter for David; *God, who is all-powerful, takes care of those who obey*, was the lesson he was learning, and he lived by it.

There were continued blessings at Saul's court. David became the favorite of the king, his armor bearer. When Saul was tormented by evil moods, he was calmed by David's music and his steady presence.

There were the heady days as popular hero, after David, armed with only a slingshot, killed the Philistine champion Goliath and brought Israel a great victory. "Saul has killed his thousands, and David his ten thousands," sang joyful women as the army came home, and though the words of the song made Saul jealous, David remained humbly aware that he was blessed by God's strength and presence and not by his own power.

There was career success, as God blessed all of David's undertakings in the army.

There were the blessings of close relationships, as David became the best friend of the king's son Jonathan and won the love of the king's daughter.

And there were even blessings in great danger, after Saul gave vent to his hatred of David and pursued him relentlessly through the wilderness. David became a fugitive, an outcast, living in caves and forests. And yet he was blessed by the loyalty and love of his companions, by the presence of God in his hardships, and by the knowledge of his own integrity.

Finally, there was the blessing of the fulfilling of God's plan, as David was anointed king of Judah and then of all Israel. There followed the taking of Jerusalem, the building of David's palace there, a victory against the Philistines, the joyous bringing of the ark of the covenant to David's city, and—best of all—a promise from God that He would forever bless David's house, guaranteeing the dynasty of David's family forever.

And then, suddenly, tragically, unexpectedly, David's life is shattered by sin. From his roof, he sees a beautiful woman bathing. Informed by his servants that it is Bathsheba, the wife of Uriah, he sends for her and sleeps with her. Later, she sends word back to him—she is pregnant. Uriah, one of David's faithful soldiers, is off fighting one of David's wars. David hatches a plan to convince him that the baby is his own. But the plan fails, and David sends a message to his commander, Joab: Put Uriah in the area of heaviest fighting and then suddenly retreat, leaving him to die. The plan works; Uriah is killed.

David's reign and life will never be the same.

[S]uddenly he is plunged into the mire, and falsifies all his past, and ruins for ever, by the sin of his mature age, his peace of heart and the prosperity of his kingdom. Thenceforward trouble is never far away; and his later years are shaded with the saddening consciousness of his great fault, as well as by hatred and rebellion and murder in his family, and discontent and alienation in his kingdom.[38]

David has become an adulterer and a murderer. Victorious through untold years of hardship, he succumbs to prosperity and laziness. Committed to his sin, he lives the next year or so utterly apart from God.

We can only imagine what this year was like for David. For perhaps the first time, he suffers a sustained period of broken fellowship with God. The man with a heart for God would find this a terribly empty time, despite the material blessings of his reign, and despite the normal joys associated with a new wife and son. Life's chief joy is suddenly absent, and whatever substitutes he is offered must seem a mockery of what he has lost. David undoubtedly found that other blessings can never fill the place in our hearts meant for God.

It must have been a hard year, too, for those around David. He could not have been the same confident, joyful person. How could he have been other than distant, unsure of himself, moody? How could his sin not have made itself known in his relations with those around him?

It's hard to imagine that his sin was much of a secret. "Who is the woman next door?" he had inquired of someone. Then he had sent messengers to have her sent to him. She, in turn, had eventually sent other messengers to him with word that she was pregnant. A certain number of both David and Bathsheba's

---

38. Alexander Maclaren, *The Life of David* (Grand Rapids: Baker Book House, 1955), 2–3.

households obviously knew of their sin; surely word of it spread from them to others throughout the city of Jerusalem.

Even more would know of the murder of Uriah. David's order to kill Uriah, communicated in a letter delivered to Joab by Uriah himself, was confidential, but its fulfillment could not have been. Everyone in Uriah's company would have known of the murder, and this story must have made its way around the kingdom.

I wonder how many times David entered a room and saw guilty looks as whispered conversations stopped. How could he have reacted? Did his face begin to turn red with embarrassment or anger? Or maybe he was able to convince himself that he was imagining things, that his secret was safe. In the end, his only response could have been to pretend he had noticed nothing. I wonder, too, how David's servants reacted to him. Did their loss of esteem for David show in their faces or their behavior? Even those who loved him must have had a hard time respecting him as before.

In the end, David's sin was found out, as sin always is. The prophet Nathan confronts David; David repents. It's a day of great sorrow and shame for David, but also a day of relief and release. The hidden is revealed. David can come out of hiding; he is forgiven.

But sin always, always has consequences. David will be punished. One day, announces Nathan, someone from within David's own household will bring violence to David's household as David had to Uriah's.

And Bathsheba's baby would die.

~

Years later, David will identify the God of blessings as the one "who redeems your life from the Pit." It's hard to imagine a pit much deeper or darker than this one: suffering the loss of your son and knowing that you alone bear the responsibility for his death. The suffering that we endure through no fault of our own is hard to take; the suffering we endure because of our own foolishness or wrongdoing is worse. And surely worst of all is seeing the suffering that our actions cause in the lives of those who have done no wrong.

David had long known that God often lets those He loves suffer. Now he learns an even more bitter truth: God even lets those He loves hurt other people. He didn't stop David from killing Uriah, a better man than himself. And He won't stop David's sin from hurting others, including his child.

But David's baby did not die to satisfy God's vengeance. There's no indication that God received any pleasure or satisfaction of justice from his death. On the contrary, in Psalm 103 David will describe God's discipline as gentle, compassionate, and merciful.[39] And he found God to be trustworthy and praiseworthy even as he was being punished.

He fasted and prayed through his child's illness, pleading with God for his baby's life. But after a week, when the baby died, David "rose from the ground, washed, anointed himself, and changed his clothes. He went into the house of the Lord, and worshiped."[40] God, David knows, is neither vengeful nor uncaring; but sin always has consequences, and David will have to live with those consequences for the rest of his life.

As he lives with the consequences, though, he also lives with a heightened sense of God's forgiveness. David has found, as Maclaren notes, that "there is a higher law of grace, whereby the sinfulness of man but draws forth the tenderness of a father's

---

39. Why, then, would David's son die? It doesn't seem right. And it isn't right, any more than it is right for a newborn baby to suffer because his mother was addicted to drugs. But the baby still suffers because sin always has consequences, both for those who sin and for others. This suffering is not right, and one day God will do away with it, as he will do away with sin.

40. 2 Samuel 12:20

pardoning pity; and the brightest revelation of His love is made to froward prodigals."[41] David's great thankfulness as he writes Psalm 103 reflects the knowledge of his guilt. As he writes, he is aware of God's favor, His blessing, His forgiveness—but yes, he remembers too his own shortcomings, his weaknesses. God has saved him from the treachery of Absalom, Shimei, Ahithophel: *The Lord works vindication and justice for all who are oppressed.* But David knows he didn't get what he deserved: *He does not deal with us according to our sins, nor repay us according to our iniquities.*

Maybe it never would have gone this far, he thinks now, in Mahanaim, *if I could just have gotten rid of Joab after he killed Abner.* He closes his eyes and looks back over the years. *Why didn't I? Was it sin, or just weakness?*

Is there a difference?

⌒

It's strange to think of David, hero and king, as a man of weaknesses. Yet he did have a chronic vulnerability: he hated confrontation. Not physical confrontation; not something simple and straightforward, like fighting a giant. That was easy. No, David's hesitancy was confrontation within his own family; he could not seem to bring himself to punish those he loved. This weakness is evident in his relationship with Joab, who was both his nephew and the commander of his army. Brave and fiercely loyal, Joab was also vengeful and violent. David publicly disapproved of Joab's crimes, yet did not punish or dismiss him.

Perhaps the saddest example of David's weakness, though, is his failure to deal with his eldest son, Amnon. Some years after the death of Bathsheba's baby, David's son Amnon "falls in love"

---

41. *Life of David*, 166.

with his half-sister Tamar; he rapes her, and then his desire turns instantly into a great loathing for her. "When David heard of all these things, he became very angry, but he would not punish his son Amnon, because he loved him, for he was his firstborn."[42] Since David will not punish Amnon, Tamar's brother Absalom takes matters into his own hands; he gains Amnon's trust with two years of patient silence, and then kills him.

Then Absalom flees, living for three years in the neighboring kingdom of Geshur. During that time, David mourns his son Amnon, but also mourns the loss of Absalom. After three years, Joab persuades the king to allow Absalom to come home. But David still does not resolve the conflict; Absalom is allowed to live in Jerusalem, but is not allowed into the king's presence. Finally, after two more years, Absalom is allowed a reunion with the king.

And then he decides to take over the kingdom for himself.

⌒

It's not necessary to go into the details of the rebellion here. David flees in disgrace, to the great joy of his enemies. He is supported by faithful friends, though, and God grants his forces the victory—only it doesn't feel like a victory, since Absalom is killed.

When word comes to David that his army was victorious but his son was killed, he mourns inconsolably. "Absalom, Absalom, my son, my son!" he cries. The victorious troops creep home in silence as they hear of his grief.

Joab is furious, and he bullies David into putting aside his mourning and greeting the troops. "It's obvious that you'd be happy now if Absalom were alive, and all your faithful friends who saved you and your family were dead," he rants. "Now, get up and greet your troops, or I swear that the end will be worse

---

42. 2 Samuel 13:21

for you than any disaster you've ever had in your life." So David does greet and thank his troops—but his heart is far away.

His son is dead, and once again he knows that it is his fault, and at many levels. Absalom's rebellion is the punishment promised by Nathan for David's sin. David must also feel that he did a poor job of raising Absalom and knows that his inability to punish either Amnon or Absalom has led him to this point. He is not aware that he is even more to blame than he thinks for Absalom's death. Before the battle, David had directed the three captains of his army to deal gently with Absalom, for his own sake. What David does not know is that Absalom was captured alive—and that Joab, a violent man whom David should have restrained years before, thrust three spears through his heart. Killing Absalom was, militarily speaking, a smart move on Joab's part. But it is a good thing for Joab that David never finds it out.

It is a good thing for David, too. The weight of the guilt he carries already is enough.

❧

David thinks now about Joab's anger with his grief. *To Joab, Absalom was a murderer and a rebel*, David thinks. *But to me, he was a son.* Nothing Absalom had done could ever have altered this truth about his identity to David. *He was my son, and I loved him.* David's breath catches as a sudden realization hits him: his thoughts for Absalom are God's thoughts for him. Others may think of David as a murderer and a rebel—and that's what he is. In murdering Uriah, he rebelled against God. And yet, to God, his identity is not, and will never be, a murderer and a rebel—he is, first and foremost, a son.

David walks to the window again and looks west, toward Jerusalem. It's strange, he thinks, that he had to leave Jerusalem in disgrace, flee across the Jordan, and lose his kingdom and his son before he could see clearly the depth of the Lord's love for him—surely beyond the depth of his own love for his own errant son. God loved David in the strength and hope of David's youthful faithfulness; He loves him no less now, an old sinful man. God's love for him, David sees now, was never about David's heart or potential or integrity; it was about a father's love for His son. *And it still is. God doesn't love me less than He did before. Though I'm disappointed in myself, God knows what I'm made of. He knew all along what was in me and what I would do, and he chose me and loved me anyway.*

Tears flow freely down David's face, and he raises his arms to God in praise:

> As the heavens are high above the earth,
>   so great is his steadfast love toward those who
>   fear him;
> as far as the east is from the west,
>   so far he removes our transgressions from us.
> As a father has compassion for his children,
>   so the Lord has compassion for those who
>   fear him.

It's easy at first to miss the depth of David's emotions as he wrote this psalm. The voice of the psalm is both calmer and quieter than many of his other psalms. Yet the times when we are crying the loudest aren't always the ones when we are suffering the most. The quietness of this psalm is caused by a greater depth of feeling, not a lesser. Alexander Maclaren's comments about Psalm 54 could very easily have been written about Psalm 103:

> The very extremity of peril has made the psalmist still and quiet . . . One feels that there is a certain self-

restraint and air of depression over the brief petitions, which indicate the depth of his distress and the uneasiness of protracted anxiety. Two notes only sound from his harp: one a plaintive cry for help; the other, thanksgiving for deliverance as already achieved.[43]

"Self-restraint" is a good description of David's tone in Psalm 103. His is not the unrestrained joy of the delivered; it is the sober joy of the forgiven. This is not, perhaps, immediately evident.

Surprisingly, Maclaren didn't perceive this self-restraint, or even an echo of distress, in Psalm 103. "There are no clouds in the horizon, nor notes of sadness in the music of this psalm," he writes. "It is well that, amid the many psalms which give voice to mingled pain and trust, there should be one of unalloyed gladness, as untouched by sorrow as if sung by spirits in heaven."[44]

More recently, Derek Kidner focuses on the same triumphant aspects of the psalm:

> Among the psalms attributed to David, Psalm 103 stands a little apart: it is less intensely personal than most of his; less harassed, if at all, by enemies or private guilt. The personal note is there, but David is soon speaking for us all. It is a hymn rather than a private thanksgiving . . .[45]

And A. F. Kirkpatrick declares that "Many Psalms which bear the name of David assume situations and circumstances wholly unlike any in which he can be supposed to have been placed, or express feelings which it is difficult to attribute to a

---

43. *Life of David*, 100.
44. "The Psalms," in *The Expositor's Bible: A Complete Exposition of the Bible*, vol. 3, ed. W. Robertson Nicoll (Baker Book House: Grand Rapids, 1982), 257.
45. *Psalms 73–150* (Downers Grove, IL: InterVarsity Press, 1978), 364.

man of his position and character . . . " Undoubtedly Psalm 103 is one of those he has in mind. He says of it, "The Psalm bears the name of David in the title, but it is impossible to suppose that it was written by him."[46] Among the evidences for his assertion are the "general style and matter of the Psalm."[47]

David would have been surprised if he could have heard on the night of Psalm 103's composition—whether in Mahanaim or somewhere else—some of the comments his psalm would one day inspire; but I think it unlikely that he would have been dismayed. His relationship with God was restored; the depth of his own sinfulness has led to a better understanding of the height of God's love; he will continue to bless the Lord, with all of his heart, for the unbelievable proportions of the unmerited blessings the Lord has provided him. As he finishes his psalm, his spirits are lifted. His determination to bless the Lord in the midst of trial has borne fruit. He is renewed.

> [T]hough the ruddy locks of the young chieftain are silvered with grey now, and sins and sorrows have saddened him, yet he can take up again with deeper meaning the tones of his old praise, and let the experience of age seal . . . the hopes of youth.[48]

---

46. *The Psalms* (Cambridge: University Press, 1957), xxxii; 599. Kirkpatrick's and Kidner's works are helpful and well written and demonstrate a scholarship far beyond any that I will ever attain. I can't help thinking, though, that they're missing some of the essence of Psalm 103.

47. "The Aramaic colouring of the language, the allusions to Job, Jeremiah, and the later chapters of Isaiah, and the general style and matter of the Psalm, combine to make it certain that it belongs to a far later date. If Ps. cii may be assigned to the close of the Exile, Ps. ciii may with equal probability be placed in the early years of the Return. It was written while the sense of the nation's forgiveness, of which that deliverance was the proof, was still fresh and vivid.

"It is evident that *vv.* 10 ff. speak of Jehovah's mercies to the nation . . ." (599–600).

48. Maclaren, *Life of David*, 257.

As the prophet Isaiah will say, thinking possibly of David's psalm,

> Those who wait for the Lord shall renew their
>   strength,
>   they shall mount up with wings like eagles,
> they shall run and not be weary,
>   they shall walk and not faint."[49]

Frank Boreham writes:

There is a touching picture in the Psalms representing David, as an old man, looking wistfully back across the years and sighing for his lost innocence. Power had come to him and eminence, but where were the simplicity and purity that were his when he kept his father's sheep? And then he magnifies the grace that has so greatly forgiven everything. A new morning has been brought out of his soul's dark night. *"My youth is renewed like the eagle's!"* he cries. He remembers how, in his early days on the grassy hillside, he watched the eagle as she built her nest, tore the down from her breast, and battered herself into ugliness in her fight for food for her young. And then the moulting season followed the breeding season. For awhile he saw her no more. And when she reappeared she was a thing of beauty and of glory, her fresh plumage glittering in the sunlight. *"My youth is renewed like the eagle's!"* he cries in a fine ecstasy. Morning had evolved from night; a fair beginning had come out of a dismal and tragic ending. Paradise Regained had followed upon Paradise Lost, and David wrote this fine song of his restored innocence.[50]

---

49. Isaiah 40:31
50. "A Faggot of Thunderbolts," in *The Golden Milestone: And Other Bric-A-Brac* (London: The Epworth Press, 1932), 30–31.

It's discouraging to read of the later years of David, a man after God's own heart, who nevertheless did not finish well. At the end of his life David would not be able to say, as the apostle Paul would nearly a thousand years later, "I have fought the good fight, I have finished the race, I have kept the faith."[51] David stumbled near the end of his race and limped home.

But he was forgiven; he was accepted; he was united with his Lord. So the lesson we learn from the end of David's life is not a lesson of his faithlessness, but a lesson of God's faithfulness: God is faithful even when we are not; nothing can separate us from His love.

In Psalm 103, David provides three illustrations of God's unlimited love—the heavens above the earth, the east from the west, a father's love for his children. God puts our sins away from us; He forgets them; He casts them into the depths of the sea.[52] This means more than just that we're separated from our sins. It means that we're separated from our identity as sinners.

Our children may grow up and do any number of bad things. But we refuse to write them off, as we're tempted to write off others. "He's a liar . . . a hypocrite . . . a killer . . ." is our judgment, and it's our final word. But our children are our children first and foremost, always. We never write off our kids, even when everyone else has. When we correct them, we know we must do it gently. If they never repent, it affects our relationship with them, but it doesn't stop us from loving them. We always give them the benefit of the doubt; we are always ready for them to come back and to forgive everything and give them another chance.

That is God's love for us, only infinitely more so. God knows us in a way that we will never know even our own chil-

---

51. 2 Timothy 4:7
52. Micah 7:19

dren. He knows us because He made us; he knows what is in us. He doesn't expect more of us than we can give; He knows our capacities. He remembers that He made us out of dust; He knows that we could crumble again like dust if He doesn't handle us gently, so gentleness is the hallmark of all His dealings with us.

You may disappoint others; you will probably be disappointed in yourself; but you will never disappoint God. God's expectations are more realistic than yours, and His love unlimited. As F. B. Meyer writes,

We do not half enough realize our Father's pity. We chastise ourselves bitterly if we do not understand or reach our ideals. We are ever fearful that He will not give us credit for the motives which underlie our sad and fitful experience. We try to make ourselves more fit for his love. And all the time He is tenderly regarding us, and knows so well how much of our failure accrues from temperament, and disposition, and overstrain.[53]

Since this is true, it is safe for us to bless Him, wise to align ourselves with His purposes.

One more important note: God faithfully fulfilled His covenant with David. There was a king from David's family on the throne in Judah until the people's rebellion against God led to their conquest by the Babylonians. Many years later, God sent another king who would rule not just Israel, but the world—Jesus Christ, born of the lineage of David.[54]

---

53. *F. B. Meyer on the Psalms: Bible Readings* (Grand Rapids: Zondervan), 124.
54. If you want to read more about the life of David, you'll find his story in 1 Samuel 16–31, all of 2 Samuel, and the first two chapters of 1 Kings.

CHAPTER 7

FLOURISHING LIKE A FLOWER: BEYOND THE BREVITY OF LIFE

AS FOR MORTALS, THEIR DAYS ARE LIKE GRASS;
  they flourish like a flower of the field;
for the wind passes over it, and it is gone,
  and its place knows it no more.

—David

A mortal, born of woman, few of days and full of
    trouble,
  comes up like a flower and withers,
  flees like a shadow and does not last.

—Job

You sweep them away; they are like a dream,
  like grass that is renewed in the morning;
  in the morning it flourishes and is renewed;
  in the evening it fades and withers.

—Moses

The grass withers, the flower fades,
  when the breath of the Lord blows upon it;
  surely the people are grass.

—Isaiah

It is always, they figure, somebody else who dies.

Only it ain't thataway. *You* can die. You can be snuffed out like you never existed at all and a few minutes after you're buried nobody will care except maybe your wife or your mother. You stick your finger in the water and you pull it out, and that's how much of a hole you leave when you're gone.

—Louis L'Amour[55]

Bad news: The experts concur, from Moses to L'Amour—you are not going to be around long, and you won't leave a single significant mark on the world to be remembered by. You are grass. Grass is pleasant enough, even pretty, but it doesn't last long and isn't terribly useful, live or dead. Nobody relaxes in the shade of a flower; it doesn't bear fruit; you don't build houses or furniture out of it.

The death of someone you love slams this news into you; you feel it deep within you, know its truth even before you can put it into words. Of course, it's been put into words already: life is fragile; life is fleeting. This is not new; you always knew it. And yet it comes somehow as a complete surprise. It's a cliché, lying dead and harmless on the floor, that suddenly jumps up and grabs you by the throat and starts squeezing.

Jerry Sittser, whose mother, wife, and young daughter were all killed in one tragic car accident, writes movingly of the experience of loss in his book *A Grace Disguised*. "At the core of loss," he says, "is the frightening truth of our *mortality*. We are creatures, made of dust." Sittser's comment echoes not only the words of King David ("We are dust. As for mortals . . ."), but

---

55. Psalm 103:15–16; Job 14:1–2; Psalm 90:5–6; Isaiah 40:7; Louis L'Amour, *The Daybreakers* (New York: Bantam Books, 1960), 24.

also of C. S. Lewis, who wrote, "No one ever told me grief felt so like fear."[56]

The frightening truth about grass is that it begs to be cut. Nicholas Wolterstorff describes his son Eric, who died in a mountain climbing accident, as "a bright flower cut down before he bloomed."[57] Your children can be cut down like flowers—like grass—and *there is nothing you can do to prevent it*. A father goes on a business trip and prays, "God, take care of my family while I'm gone"—as if he were the one taking care of them when he is home. *Only it ain't thataway.* It may not seem like it to him, but the safety of his family is almost entirely out of his control.

No one feels the immediacy of this fact like someone who has lost a child. A few months after Allison's death, a friend and I were talking about the comfort offered by Psalm 103. "His righteousness is to your children's children," pointed out my friend, citing verse 17.

"Frankly," I said quietly, "I still have trouble reading that verse."

"Why is that?" he asked, surprised.

"Because Allison is not going to have any children."

━━━

The news gets worse before it gets better. The flowers that live out their lives don't fare much better than those cut down. They bloom briefly, then wither and die. And to make matters worse, the bloom is rarely as impressive as anticipated.

For some reason, this also comes as a surprise. It's this surprise that triggers what we call a midlife crisis. It's not as dramatic a crisis as a death in the family, of course, but it can be hard to work through nonetheless. We may be resigned to our lives being a flash in the pan, but it's still disconcerting to see

---

56. *A Grief Observed* (New York: Seabury Press, 1961), 7.
57. *Lament for a Son* (Grand Rapids: Wm. B. Eerdmans, 1987), 40.

how tiny of a flash it was. At about the time we were expecting the bloom to begin to truly open up, we suddenly notice it's not getting any bigger at all; and then to our dismay, it starts to fade. We see suddenly that our bloom isn't going to be anywhere near as bright, or last as long, as we had thought. "I am never going to reach my potential," we realize, and the thought can cause something of a panic.

Interestingly, David doesn't even mention the withering of the grass. He doesn't say we fade like the flower of the field, but that we *flourish* like that flower. It's not just the fading of life that's sad, not just the coming of old age with its limitations and unrealized expectations. No, even the triumphs of the strength of our youth, our successes, our glories, are as nothing. It's as if David is saying, "You won't reach your potential, but don't let it bother you—your potential wasn't all that great anyway."

David talks like someone who knows sorrow. As I listen to those who have suffered great loss, I hear, over and over again, the same thoughts that occurred to me: "Is there any meaning? In a world where something like this can happen, does anything matter?" David must have asked the same question; and his conclusion is that if there is going to be any meaning at all in this world, it will have to be supplied by God himself.

Set against the brevity and insignificance of human life and endeavor is the eternal, immortal, unchanging, steadfast love of the almighty God. This steadfast love "is from everlasting to everlasting on those who fear him." This means more than simply that God has always responded with love toward those who fear Him. It means that if you fear God, He has been preparing His blessings for you and shaping your life from before the beginning of time—and has put just as much love into shaping and blessing your future, and the future of your children. God's steadfast love is poured out on you as your bloom is fading, even as when it was meaninglessly flourishing.

I'm not sure how you normally work your way through a midlife crisis. My own, with which I struggled for years, was ended mercilessly by Allison's death. Not that I'm no longer bothered by unrealized expectations or by my shortcomings as a father, husband, pastor, friend; but those disappointments have themselves become comparatively inconsequential, made so not only by Allison's death but by the steadfast love of the Lord.

I will never reach what I thought was my potential. My influence on the world will be small. I have no control over dangers to my family or over my own destiny. And Allison, cut down before she could bloom, will never have any children. But to my great relief, I find that I can let those things go; they are already, in fact, in the hands of the eternal God, who loves me and who from eternity has been shaping His eternal plan for me and for Allison.

Your life may not make a good deal of difference to the world, but it has infinite importance to God. He didn't create you so you could wither and die, but so you could enjoy Him forever. The end of your life on earth is not the end; it's just the end of your existence as grass. The brevity of that existence, as it turns out, is a good thing, for what follows is far more fulfilling and substantial.

HOW COMPLETELY SATISFYING to turn from our limitations to a God who has none. Eternal years lie in his heart. For him, time does not pass, it remains; and those who are in Christ share with him all the riches of limitless time and endless years.

A. W. Tozer, *The Knowledge of the Holy*[58]

---

58. A. W. Tozer, *The Knowlege of the Holy* (San Francisco: HaperCollins, 1992), 64.

DAVID'S FRIEND MOSES

IN MANY WAYS, PSALM 103 IS A COMPANION TO Psalm 90, a psalm traditionally attributed to Moses, who lived some six hundred years before David. David addresses in a new way some of the same themes explored by Moses, so the two psalms complement each other beautifully.

PSALM 90

Lord, you have been our dwelling place in all
    generations.
Before the mountains were brought forth,
    or ever you had formed the earth and the world,
    from everlasting to everlasting you are God.
You turn us back to dust,
    and say, "Turn back, you mortals."
For a thousand years in your sight are like yesterday
when it is past,
    or like a watch in the night.
You sweep them away; they are like a dream,
    like grass that is renewed in the morning;
in the morning it flourishes and is renewed;
    in the evening it fades and withers.
For we are consumed by your anger;
    by your wrath we are overwhelmed.
You have set our iniquities before you,
    our secret sins in the light of your countenance.
For all our days pass away under your wrath;
    our years come to an end like a sigh.

The days of our life are seventy years, or perhaps eighty,
if we are strong;
    even then their span is only toil and trouble;
        they are soon gone, and we fly away.
Who considers the power of your anger?
    Your wrath is as great as the fear that is due you.
So teach us to count our days that we may gain a wise
    heart.
Turn, O Lord! How long?
    Have compassion on your servants!
Satisfy us in the morning with your steadfast love,
    so that we may rejoice and be glad all our days.
Make us glad as many days as you have afflicted us,
    and as many years as we have seen evil.
Let your work be manifest to your servants,
    and your glorious power to their children.
Let the favor of the Lord our God be upon us,
    and prosper for us the work of our hands—
        O prosper the work of our hands!

CHAPTER 8

DEVELOPING ROOTS: DOWN SYNDROME AND SCARS IN HEAVEN

I WANT TO MOVE AWAY FROM LOOKING DIRECTLY at Psalm 103 for a chapter or two, but I don't plan to move far from its themes of blessing, comfort, and hope.

When I was in college there was a blind student, Tod, living in my dorm. Tod had an amazing ability to thrive in his surroundings despite his lack of sight. One day a friend of mine was walking with Tod from the dining hall to the classroom and was just about to warn him about a mud puddle they were approaching when Tod reached out and gave my friend a playful shove, nearly sending him into the puddle. How did he know—? "Oh, I found out pretty early in the semester that there's always a puddle there in wet weather," Tod explained.

Though blind, Tod was probably a lot more in tune to the world around him than those of us with all five of our senses. He had to be. It's not that he had super-human abilities, but in order to survive, he had to develop some potential that lies dormant in the rest of us for all of our lives.

Tragedy has a similar effect on us.

Tragedy sharpens our thinking about God; it demands that we think things through; it forces us to re-evaluate what we had previously accepted without examination. It's a refining fire that burns away the dross, a time of drought that obliges us to extend our roots deeper and in new directions. It can become a rich time as we find and confirm solid truths and jettison erroneous assumptions.

Allison's death forced me into fresh thinking about life, about suffering, about God. I wouldn't go so far as to say that because of Allison's death, I know more about God than you do, but I won't hesitate to affirm that because of her death, I know more about God than I did.

There are aspects of my theology that never got a lot of exercise until recently. One of these is my understanding of people born with handicaps—specifically, those with Down syndrome.

I've already mentioned that my youngest daughter, Andrea, has Down syndrome. Now, I've lost a daughter, and I've had a daughter born with Down syndrome, and the experiences are not as different as you might think. I was struck by the similarities as I read Mark Buchanan's account of the death of a young man in his church. The emotions this young man's mother experienced are typical for a grieving parent, but interestingly, they are also typical for the parent of a newborn with Down syndrome.

> The hardest thing for her has been letting go of the dreams she had for her son. She wanted to be there when he fell in love, when he came home to announce he was engaged, when he stood at the head of the church and watched his bride walk down the aisle. She wanted to see what God was going to do with his gift of leadership and his love for children.[59]

---

59. *The Holy Wild*, (Sisters, OR: Multnomah Press, 2003), 50.

I've experienced the heartache of letting go of those dreams twice now.

The day of Andrea's birth was one of terrible, gut-wrenching emotions for my wife and me—another day when our lives and our perspective on all of life changed. This is also a typical response, though not universal. I've since met a few sets of parents who were not thrown off balance at all by the birth of their special baby. These people were just as happy and proud as they would have been with the birth of a "normal" baby.

It wasn't that easy for me. I was a mangled wreck of emotions. Until Andrea (our sixth child), the emotions I associated with having a new baby were intense happiness and pride. Andrea's birth was different. It's a strange, hollow feeling to have had a baby and not really want to share that news with anyone. It's not that I was ashamed of her; I just had a hard time getting through the exchange:

"My wife had a baby girl the other day."

"Great! Everybody doing okay?"

"Well, the baby's still in the hospital with a blood infection, but she'll recover from that. And, well, she has Down syndrome. . ."

And then they wouldn't know how to react, and I wouldn't know how to make them feel more comfortable. I thought about sharing my news without mentioning Down syndrome; but I didn't want anybody to think I was trying to hide it, either.

Meanwhile, we were still trying to deal with it ourselves— or make deals with God about it. "God, I see now that I never had much compassion for the disabled or paid much attention to them. I'm changed now; I've learned my lesson. Now, if you'd just heal Andrea, please? Just have the doctor call us up and tell us the test was negative, it was just a false alarm." But God wasn't negotiating.

Giving up our dreams for Andrea caused us great heartache. But raising her has been a challenge, a joy, and an education. She has had a tremendous impact on our lives. She's increased our capacity for compassion, she's slowed us down, she's given us a lot of extra work. She has also stretched our view of God's ways and His will.

With Allison's death, Andy lost her best friend. But she has never showed that it bothered her. Andy's family had already grown a little smaller when her older sister, Anna, went off to college. We all wondered how Andy would take Anna's departure: Would she miss her? Would she cry? Would she be able to understand our explanations of why Anna wasn't around anymore? We were a little surprised—and Anna maybe a little disappointed—to find that Andy wasn't bothered much at all by Anna's absence. To Andy, Anna's being out of the room and Anna's being on a different continent mean exactly the same thing.

She has reacted the same way to Alli's absence. She loves looking at pictures of Allison, as she loves looking at pictures of herself. She hasn't forgotten Alli—she quickly identifies her in the pictures. But she never asks where Alli is, what happened to her, when she'll see her again. Perhaps she is unable to ask, or maybe is unable even to formulate that sort of concept in her head. Maybe someday she will. But for now, at least, it's a relief that she can't, or doesn't. So far, the only time I've been really grateful for Andy's Down syndrome is when it meant that I didn't have to explain to my four-year-old why she would never see her sister again in this world.

So far.

But as I started to say, my theology about Down syndrome has changed quite a bit. Before Andy, I thought the Bible was clear on the theology of the handicapped. The Bible tells us that we suffer because of sin. There are hard times in our lives in this world because the world is broken. "The whole creation has been groaning in labor pains until now," and we all groan with it, as we wait for Christ to return to the world and set things right.[60] Andy wasn't born with Down syndrome because of her sin or that of her parents, but because when sin entered the world, suffering entered as well. Some suffering exists as a result of personal sin and the loving discipline of God in our lives; other suffering—that caused by hurricanes or cyclones or old age or birth defects—just happens. Sin messes things up; it has caused a lot of suffering in a lot of lives, including in the lives of those special kids born with disabilities. God can, and does, use those unfortunate events to shape our lives and characters and turn all things to our good, but that doesn't change the fact that the events themselves are the result of a fallen world.

I always knew that this was a delicate subject for those families of children with disabilities and should be addressed with care. My father worked for many years at a Christian high school, and he told me once about how upset a student became when her Bible teacher explained that suffering—and thus handicaps—were the result of sin. The student's brother had Down syndrome, and she refused to accept the idea that his condition was the result of sin. To her, her brother was what he was, and she wouldn't trade him or change him or dismiss his uniqueness as a result of Satan's work in the world. Her love for her brother was commendable, but the Bible is pretty clear about this: a world without sin is a world without suffering. No sin, no Down syndrome.

That's what I believed before.

I've had some time to think about it since then. Six years of thinking about it, as a matter of fact. And while I haven't come to a lot of definite conclusions, I have seen that my theology

60. Romans 8:22

was stunted, atrophied. The answers were clear to me because I had never had the necessity of questioning them.

When Andrea was born, I would have given anything to take away her Down syndrome. We grieved for all the problems we knew she would have: the taunts from other children, the learning disabilities, the fact that she would never have her own children, never live on her own. I would have given anything to restore my daughter's future. My right arm? Of course. My own life? Gladly.

I would still give my life for my daughter, or for any of my kids. But my understanding of her Down syndrome has changed significantly. I realized this as I read a newspaper article not too long ago, an interview with a college basketball player who referred to a new friend as "a victim of Down syndrome."

I read that line to Andrea's seventeen-year-old brother, Nate, and asked him what he thought of it. His initial reaction was the same as mine: a *victim* of Down syndrome? What a silly way to put it. Andrea is Andrea. And I was genuinely surprised to suddenly realize that not only did I love Andy the way she was, but that I wouldn't take away her Down syndrome if I could. Andrea is not a victim of Down syndrome; it's just part of her. It's who she is, and we love her that way.

I remember playing with Andy the day I realized this. She was smiling the same as always, but her smile hit me in a special way. I felt almost like she was understanding that I understood. "So you finally get it!" her smile said to me.[61]

But what about the theology? Sure, my love for Andy is commendable, but isn't the Bible clear on this? No sin, no suffering, no Down syndrome.

---

61. My wife, who spends a lot more time with Andy than I do, has a different perspective. She would not yet, and may never, say that she wouldn't take away Andrea's Down syndrome if she could. I would be less than surprised if it turns out that, as usual, she's right.

Well, no. The Bible is clear, yes; but it clearly does not assert the things I thought it did. Here are the things that were clear to me before:

- If sin had never entered the world, no children would be born handicapped.
- Their condition, and that of the world, will one day be remedied. When we get to heaven, no one will be handicapped. The deaf will hear, and the blind will see. The mentally disabled will be as intelligent as anyone—or more so!

I was almost right.

But these conclusions, though not necessarily wrong, are not as certain as I once assumed. Take, for example, the idea that Andrea's intelligence will be much greater in heaven. Not just the Bible but even our own experience should prevent us from insisting that this is necessarily so.

Which of us believes that the happiest, most well-balanced and fulfilled—or even the most successful—people in this life are those who are the most intelligent? Probably all of us know some very intelligent people who are unable, in spite of or even because of their high I.Q., to relate to those around them. Many intelligent people are deeply unhappy. And while that may not be a good reason for the rest of us to congratulate each other on being stupid, it should give us a clue that a sparkling intellect may not be a necessary aspect of our perfect lives in heaven.

Will we know more in heaven? Certainly. Our perspective of life from heaven will give us a much better comprehension of the meaning of life. Will we know God better and understand His will more fully? Sure we will; we'll be with Him. Today we know in part; then, we will have a perfect knowledge of God (though of course we will never have a complete understanding of His infinite being). Will we all possess a super-intelligence above that which we have here on earth? There's no reason to conclude that it must be so.

If you're unconvinced, let's examine the question from another angle. Do you think that in heaven all of us will have exactly the same level of intelligence? I don't think anyone I know would say yes. Even if we all are much smarter than we are here on earth, there's no reason to assume that we will not continue to glorify God by the great variety of our personalities and gifts. Some of us will be more artistic, some perhaps more athletic, some better at thinking through complex mathematical equations. And if that's so, how can we believe that in a perfect world a high I.Q. is necessary? After all, if the average intelligence in heaven is earth's equivalent of 300, wouldn't the person with an I.Q. of 250 be "handicapped"?

And even if our I.Q. is twice that, would it mean that we were any closer to appreciating or understanding the infinite being of God? No! The distance between our finite minds and His infinite mind will always be an unfathomable, unbridgeable distance. *And this is no more true for the profoundly mentally handicapped than it is for the world's foremost theologian.* I have to think that compared to God, all of us here on earth are at basically the same intellectual level. There is certainly a much greater distance between my intellectual capacity and God's than between mine and Andrea's. The intellectual distance between us and God is not unlike (and perhaps greater than) the distance between us and insects. And when was the last time you looked at an ant hill and thought to yourself, "Hey, there's a really tall ant. I'll bet it would be a lot easier for me to relate personally to that tall ant than it would with all those other little ants"?

Yes, there is a difference. Insects are not created in our image, while we are created in the image of God. And if you don't think too deeply about that concept, you'll see that our ability to reason is part of what being made in the image of God means; our reasoning capacity is one of the things that separate us from animals, who are not made in the image of God. And if you're not really careful, the thought will then slip into your theology that the mentally handicapped thus reflect more dimly the image of God and are in more dire need of repair.

But Andrea is not created less in the image of God than I am. Indeed, I wonder sometimes if her Down syndrome may one day—if not now—allow her to appreciate some aspects of God's character that are veiled to me by my "intelligence." What if her condition includes with it the ability to draw closer to God?

What if it was God's will from the beginning of eternity to create some of His children with Down syndrome, even if the world had never fallen from grace?

This is a thought that never would have occurred to me seven years ago, and I suspect that if anyone had suggested it, I would have dismissed it quickly. Look at the life of people with Down syndrome, after all; they are unable to live on their own, take care of themselves, protect themselves, or function adequately in their world.

But independence is overrated—if, indeed, there is such a thing. It is true that people with Down syndrome can't protect themselves in the world. (Can anyone, really?) In a perfect world, though, they would have no need of protection—or, possibly, of any kind of independence. Perhaps heaven will contain a lot of people with Down syndrome for us to serve and help and learn from. Perhaps the presence of people with Down syndrome in this world is one of God's blessings—a group of people uniquely qualified to teach us the value of mutual dependence, love, care, patience.

Maybe the fall didn't cause Down syndrome; maybe it just caused it to be a handicap. Perhaps Down syndrome doesn't *exist* because of sin, but is a *handicap* because of sin.

Maybe we should even wonder if it's *Andy's* body that's inadequate. After all, she does have an extra chromosome in every cell in her body, a chromosome that you and I do not possess. Perhaps that chromosome has a tremendously important purpose that we don't as yet comprehend. This seems more than a little unlikely, I admit. I guess I don't really think that in heaven we'll all be repaired and enjoy the chromosome we're missing so badly—the one that allows us to feel our emotions more freely, to love uninhibitedly, to think without thinking we're smarter than God.

But I wouldn't bet against it, either.

⌒

This whole business of what heaven is like is another aspect of my theology that has gotten a lot of exercise lately. I've often heard it said that when we get there, things will be so wonderful that we'll forget our trials here on earth. But I've seen in the Bible lately some good indications that this is not so.

According to the Bible, those who believe in Christ will live in heaven not just as spirits (like the angels), but in resurrected bodies as well. It offers only two bits of information about those bodies, though. It hints that they won't resemble our human bodies much more than the oak resembles the acorn. And it tells us that those bodies will be like Christ's:

> He will transform the body of our humiliation that it
> may be conformed to the body of his glory . . .[62]

---

62. Philippians 3:21

Beloved, we are God's children now; what we will be
has not yet been revealed. What we do know is this:
when he is revealed, we will be like him, for we will see
him as he is.[63]

What we know about Christ's glorified body, though, is fairly limited. We know that it was a physical body, though not like ours. He ate and drank, but He could also materialize through locked doors and disappear from before the eyes of those who were with Him. We know that some of His best friends didn't recognize him at first. And we know that His shiny, brand new, fresh-out-of-the-box body was scarred.

"Come," He told Thomas. "Touch the nail prints in my hands. Reach out and put your hand in my side."

Jesus will not suffer in heaven; there will be no need for Him ever to be offered again for sins. But the evidence of His suffering remains for all eternity.

Why? We can only suppose that the scars are left on His body because they give glory to God. The price that Christ paid to redeem the world will never be forgotten.

And if that is true, is it possible that our own hardships will be remembered as well? It's a great encouragement to me to think that they will be. If we carry our scars with us to heaven, then every physical trial we undergo here on earth for God's glory will continue to give Him glory forever.

Five times the apostle Paul received thirty-nine lashes; three times he was beaten with rods; once he was stoned. When I see Him in heaven, I won't be surprised if His new body carries marks from those beatings.

It's taken me awhile to get used to this idea. As far as I thought of heaven at all in the past forty years, I think I've

---

63. 1 John 3:2

always pictured it as being full of stunningly beautiful people. Scars don't really fit that picture. But now that I think of it, I don't suppose that the scars on Jesus' body make it any less appealing. Perhaps the big difference in heaven will not be that we're so much better looking but that we will have a much more accurate sense of true beauty.

If Paul's glorified body bears scars, we can be sure that they will be scars that make him more attractive and give glory to the God he served here on earth.

⌒

My friends Kevin and Kay Ann miss their son Timothy greatly. But they know that one day they'll see him again. And when they do, he won't have tubes sticking into his body; he won't be too tired to stand; his body won't be bloated from medication.

But I wonder if he won't carry scars from his illness—scars that bear witness to the testimony he gave for God by his faithful suffering for Him here. Beautiful scars, bright reminders that announce God's goodness and faithfulness for all eternity.

And if that's possible—if our glorified bodies, like Christ's, could bear eternal witness of God's faithfulness in our earthly physical trials—perhaps they will give evidence of our emotional trials as well. Maybe Kevin and Kay Ann's heavenly bodies will bear witness to the glory they brought to God through their faithful trust in Him through the earthly heartache of Timothy's cancer. I'm not sure how.

Maybe the crowns they receive will be part of their bodies.

Or maybe the scars on their hearts will be somehow visible to the rest of us.

None of us would choose to suffer. But in our suffering, we can choose to suffer for God.

I believe that suffering has eternal value. I believe that every smile that Timothy shared with the doctors and nurses and every minute that Kevin and Kay Ann chose to trust in God, though their hearts were being ripped apart, were both earthly testimonies to God's grace and acts that will give God glory forever.

The scars on Christ's hands tell me so.

CHAPTER 9

COMFORTING THE SUFFERING: VACANT CHAFF WELL MEANT FOR GRAIN

TRAGEDY ALWAYS COMES AS A SURPRISE.

Maybe that's because we normally learn about suffering when it's somebody else doing the actual suffering. A change in perspective makes all the difference in the world.

I think I first took notice of this truth while fishing on a party boat in the Gulf of Mexico. The trip began with a two-hour voyage to international waters. Since the sea was a bit rough, by the time the actual fishing started nearly all of us had begun suffering from seasickness, to varying degrees. The person who suffered most was a boy who started feeling a bit nauseated thirty minutes offshore and spent most of the next six hours at the side of the boat vomiting, recovering from vomiting, and getting ready to vomit.

His father was one of the few on the boat not affected by the waves. I'll never forget the sight of the boy sitting with his head in his hands near the side of the boat and his father sitting next to him with a sandwich in one hand and a fishing pole in the other. "Why don't you try fishing for awhile?" he urged his son. "Maybe it will take your mind off it."

A lot of the things we say to grieving people are like that.

Missionary Paul Stock writes of his struggles after the death of his brother:

> A group of people walked towards me and one woman took my hands. "So sorry to hear about your brother's passing, but we know he's in a better place," she said. Better for whom? His wife? His children? Another hugged me. "God likes to take the good people home to be with him," the person muttered. So we're the rotten ones? Again, "You'll see him again in heaven." But what do I do now? And again, "Maybe God was saving him from an even worse death." How do you know? People cared and wanted to help, but I wished they would just give me a hug.[64]

"How little impression our sorrow makes upon other men," observed Andrew Bonar.[65] *It's sad, but we know he's in a better place.*

"We all have strength enough to endure the troubles of others," noticed the Duke de la Rochefoucauld. *God needed her with him more than we needed her here.*

"The heart knows its own bitterness, and no stranger shares its joy," says Proverbs 14:10. *It must be a comfort that you have five other healthy children.*

Perhaps fishing will take your mind off it.

↜

Job's friends were that kind of comforter. Surely no one ever suffered more thoroughly or dramatically than did Job. He not only lost everything he had—including his ten children—in

---

64. "Reflections on the Life of Dale," *Evangelical Missions Quarterly* 42 (January 2006): 60–65.
65. *Diary and Letters* (London: Hodder and Stoughton), 192.

a single day, he lost it all under such obviously supernatural circumstances that everyone understood that God had a hand in his calamity. What they didn't know was that while God was indeed involved, He was on Job's side. He had given Satan permission to attack Job in order to prove to Satan that Job's goodness was not dependent on the blessings God had given him—and, it seems, in order to deepen Job's relationship with his God.

It's understandable, perhaps, that Job's friends assumed that his downfall was punishment for some terrible sin. If they had known the true cause of Job's suffering, perhaps they would have been better comforters.

But I doubt it. What if they had known about God's conversations with Satan and were able to share them with Job? "So you see, Job," they could have assured him, "everything is okay. It's all part of God's will for your life." Do you suppose that would have been a great comfort to Job?

I picture him blinking uncomprehendingly at hearing this news. "What? My kids have all been killed, my reputation destroyed, my wealth taken, and my body covered with painful sores, so that God could win a bet? That's supposed to make me feel better? He couldn't have just bet on the camel races or something?"

Instead, Job's comfort comes from God himself, who finally shows up on the scene and answers all of Job's questions by basically saying, "Who are you to ask? I'm God; you're not." And Job, perhaps to our surprise, is completely satisfied—not by theological answers, but by the presence of God. God's rebuke is for Job a hug of reassurance. That the Creator and Ruler of the universe cares enough about him to speak to him personally is all the answer and comfort that he requires. It is enough.

But you are not God, so a rebuke from you to those who are grieving would probably not be much comfort. What can you say, then, if you would avoid being like Job's comforters? How can you be sure that you can come up with something that doesn't hurt rather than help? You'd rather not say anything at all than say something that would add to the heartache; but sometimes saying nothing is not an option. And you do care, so you'd like to say something that would help. So what would be an appropriate response? What do suffering people want?

I haven't been elected as a spokesman for the suffering, but I'll offer my opinion anyway: what we want is better theology, and less of it.

We'll start with the need for less: The day of tragedy is not an appropriate time for theological discussion.

If a friend of yours was kicked in the head by a horse, what do you suppose would be the appropriate response? Would you want him to know that God loves him even in this hard time? As he sits on the ground dizzy, stunned, with the breath knocked out of him, would you quickly move to assure him that the blow he has sustained is encompassed in the sovereign and perfect will of a God who loves him, that because of this blow he will become a better person, and that God must have something special in mind for his life plan if He would allow this sort of suffering to be a part of it?

No, it's likely that you'd know instinctively that what your friend needs most (with the possible exception of medical attention!) is a hug, a reassuring hand, your patient presence.

One day down the road, he may desire to pursue the metaphysical implications of the hoof print in his head. Perhaps you'll even be able to help him work through that. But don't be in a hurry; the time will come, but this is not it. For now, a hug is the only theology he needs. He's not ready for deep discussion.

Sudden loss is a kick in the head; treat it like one.

The other reason you should hesitate to share your thoughts on suffering with grieving friends is that they may already understand it better than you do, may be experiencing it at a level you have not, may be asking better questions and demanding better answers. It's not that the information you have to offer is necessarily wrong; it just may not be relevant. Maybe you should be listening to your friend instead of offering advice.

The visitor to the zoo's reptile house and the man in the jungle who wakes up to find a python squeezing the life out of him both know something true about snakes, but only one of them is actively engaged with that truth. One's knowledge is theoretical, the other's frighteningly practical.

If you've suffered in the way your friend is suffering, though, feel free to share what you've learned. Kay Ann, whose son Timothy had been fighting cancer for five years, told us, "We have learned that God is good." That statement coming from her was very meaningful. The same words coming from friends who had not lost a family member were no less true, but they lacked the weight of personal experience.

Our friends supported us in the best way possible. Many sent us a simple card with a single Bible verse. I don't remember which verses. They probably knew that the verse might not help much, but they also knew that we'd want to hear from them. They were right.

Many others said something like, "We're not even going to try to quote a Bible verse to you. We just want you to know that we love you and we're praying for you." They were right too.

Many, many said, "I know I can't even imagine the pain you're going through." Yes, they were right.

Consolation from those who had suffered as we had was always welcome, even when they offered advice or theology that didn't comfort us in the way it had comforted them.

I don't remember which responses came from which friends. I've saved them somewhere, and maybe someday I'll go back through them. For now, though, it's enough to know that our friends and family were there for us, that they were standing by when we needed them, and that they were thinking of and praying for us. These responses were appropriate and appreciated. Their words were a verbal hug, a short embrace.

∽

Is there anything outside of a hug that you can offer?

Sure. Don't underestimate the importance of helping out in mundane tasks like offering meals, taking care of children, running errands, helping with financial needs, preparing the memorial service. There are a thousand and one details to be attended to in a crisis, and those stricken with grief may have barely enough energy to get out of bed.

We were blessed greatly by the way our family, colleagues, friends, and neighbors took care of us when we couldn't take care of ourselves. In our dazed state, I'm sure we forgot many of these kindnesses immediately, and there were undoubtedly countless others of which we were never aware. These things matter. We remain grateful.

It's always appropriate to listen.

It's helpful to share something specific about the personality of the person who died.

As bad as I felt for a long time after Allison's death, my primary worry was never whether I would feel better. I was terrified that I would forget—forget Allison's face, her voice, her personality; afraid that everything that made Allison what she was would be lost to me and to the world forever.

And so the responses that I treasure most of all are stories about Allison that I hadn't heard before, stories that painted her personality more clearly, maybe in ways that were new to me; stories that illustrated her beauty.

There weren't very many of those. Many people said, "Allison was such a special person. She was so loving," which was good to hear, but wasn't enough. There were a few people, though, who could say things like, "Do you know, Allison was in my Sunday school class, and every week she . . ."

If you can, tell the grieving a personal story that reveals a special quality of the person they're missing. It will be greatly appreciated.

Mark the day on your calendar. Write back in six months to let us know you're still praying for us.

Pray for us.

Write to us during the holidays, or on the anniversary of her death, or on her birthday. Tell us you haven't forgotten her.

Don't forget her.

❧

Since I've elected myself spokesman for the grieving, I'll share as well a few brief thoughts on what I consider inappropriate responses.

Sympathetic notes from friends, whether long or short, were as welcome as hugs from them. Long, theologically top-heavy letters from people we didn't know, though—unless they came from others who had suffered deeply—were not helpful. We didn't receive many of these, perhaps two or three. We found them intrusive rather than helpful, not unlike the long, rocking hug Jodi endured from a total stranger at the hospital on the day Allison died. A year and a half later, she ran into the woman at a church she was visiting. "I'm sure you don't remember me," the woman said, "I was in the hospital the day . . ." Oh, yes. I remember you.

What can you do if the family who has suffered a loss is one with which you have not been on the best of terms? Perhaps the tragedy has made you realize that whatever was behind your disagreement is nothing in comparison with the tragedy suffered. You may feel the need to take this opportunity to clear the air and restore the broken relationship.

Please don't. Be at the service. Say, "I'm so sorry." Stay in the background. This is not about you. If you are truly sorry for past actions and disputes, you'll have a chance someday to make it right. But not today. The family who is hurting has neither the energy nor the motivation to suddenly let you back into their good graces. They have more important things to think about, if they can think at all.

One day last summer I shared our grief and our experiences with a group of fellow missionaries. One woman there shared one of hers. Years earlier, her husband was in critical condition in the hospital, apparently on his deathbed. He was heavily drugged and in and out of consciousness. And at his bedside came a trickling stream of estranged family members and friends who wanted to "make their peace" with him, so that when he died, they wouldn't feel there were unsettled issues.

The woman went to a family member and told him, "Get these vultures out of here. If they want to make things right with him, let them do it after he recovers, when he's conscious and healed."

They left.

The man recovered.

None of those people came back to see him.

Don't try to wrap up the meaning of suffering in a sound bite so we can get on with life. Don't tell me it's God's will;

don't tell me God is good. I don't find these statements offensive, I just don't find them comforting—unless, like Kay Ann, you're sharing what you know from a depth of personal experience. I've thought about this a lot and have come to two conclusions:

I believe that God is good.

I don't believe that it's appropriate for you to tell me so when my daughter dies.

When my daughter dies, it's *my* job to tell *you* that God is good. Until I can do that, don't be like Job's friends. Offer your support, and wait in silence.

Don't try to make the pain go away. The pain doesn't go away. Hurt with me.

Last spring the twenty-two-year-old daughter of some friends of ours was struck and killed by a car. Her boyfriend was planning to take her to see her parents that weekend and propose to her. We sent our friends a short note, knowing that nothing we could say would help and knowing too that they were overwhelmed, but wanting to let them know we were thinking of them.

We got an even shorter note back: "Does it ever get better? I'm wondering how to get through this?"

Here's part of my reply:

Dear John & Lynn,

Does it ever get better? Yes, there will come a time when it's not so hard. It will be easier to breathe, to think, to sleep. The pain becomes—well—not less, but less sharp.

Does it ever stop hurting? No—don't worry. It doesn't. You will never forget Mandy or forget how you feel today, not if you live another eighty years. There will never be a day that passes that you won't be a different person because of the effect her life and her death has had on you. You will become more in touch with the suffering around you, more affectionate, more dependent on God, less absorbed in the petty wrangling and insignificant necessities of life. The changes in you will be almost uniformly positive—and you would give them all away gladly, if you could, in exchange for five minutes more with your daughter.[66]

Another friend recently shared her family's story with me.

My sister Patty was three years old when she died. My dad had gotten out of the car to take back to the store some milk bottles (glass back then), but had forgotten to bring the bottles. My mom grabbed the bottles to take them to him and come right back. In a split second, Patty opened the back door (the handles went down back then) and ran into traffic and was hit by a car. This was in 1924. The driver was devastated and took my dad and Patty to the hospital in Grand Rapids. She died in my dad's arms from internal hemorrhaging.

When I was packing for college, I came across a box of clothes with dried blood on them. I called my mother upstairs and she started crying. She had saved Patty's clothes from the accident all these years. When I came back home for a weekend, mom had already gotten rid of them.

My dad died at seventy-eight years old in 1978. I was with him when he took his last breath. He told me, "I'm going

---

66. It's quite possible that while composing the letter I was unconsciously quoting from Nicholas Wolterstorff's *Lament for a Son*: "I have changed, yes. For the better, I do not doubt. But without a moment's hesitation I would exchange those changes for Eric back" (73).

to see my little Patty now." My mother died when she was eighty-four. When she was dying, she said, "I don't care to live on this earth any longer. I just want to see Patty again."

The pain doesn't ever go away. You don't get through this; you never recover. Like the scars on Jesus' hands, the pain is always there.

It wouldn't be love if it weren't.

∽

No, praise the Lord, the pain does not ever go away. The pain means you're alive, and you remember; sometimes it even means you're more connected with the world around you. Every time those around you hurt, the scars on your heart resonate with a similar pain, like the sympathetic harmony of the strings on a violin when a corresponding note is played on a nearby piano.

This is a good thing. Until Christ returns to install a kingdom without death and pain, the next best thing is for us to feel the pain of others when they're hurting.

BLESSED BE the God and Father of our Lord Jesus Christ, the Father of mercies and the God of all consolation, who consoles us in all our affliction, so that we may be able to console those who are in any affliction with the consolation with which we ourselves are consoled by God.[67]

I've been wondering lately what kind of comforter Job became. Surely, having experienced suffering and comfort to the extent that he did, he must have known how to offer comfort to those around him.

---

67. 2 Corinthians 1:3–4

But I don't think the comfort he offered would have been accomplished by theological proposition, by explication of suffering's causes and implications. It's interesting to note that some of the lessons we glean on the theology of suffering from the book of Job would probably never have occurred to Job himself; as far as we know, Job was never told why he had suffered. "Despite it all, God is God; and He cares for me," is about the extent of what he could say he'd learned.

Yet the depth to which he'd experienced that truth! A fathomless depth, impossible to express. I don't think Job could have put into words all that he gained through God's comfort; but I don't think that inability would make him any less sure of it.

I imagine that the thing Job could not explain—the comfort of the presence of God—became the motivation for him to become the best possible comforter. And while he could not offer God's presence, he could offer his own. Job's unhelpful friends, to their credit, sat with Job for a week in silence before offering their advice. I think Job would have known how to wait longer—as long as was necessary.

And I think he probably gave the gentlest, most reassuring hugs in all the country.

DAVID'S FRIEND JOB

WE'RE NOT SURE WHEN Job lived, perhaps in the days of Abraham, David's ancestor. This would put him some fifteen hundred years before David's time. Nonetheless, despite the years separating them, it seems to me that Job is the friend David might have felt closest to as he wrote Psalm 103.

For most of the book of Job, we see Job as a righteous man who had a lot more questions than answers. G. Campbell Morgan has pointed out that the most complete answers to Job's questions are provided in the life and work of Jesus Christ. *The Answers of Jesus to Job* was the name of his book on the subject.

Equally appropriate—if perhaps not as definitive—would be a book called *Psalm 103: The Answers of David to Job.* In fact, if David had set out to answer in brief the questions Job addresses at length, he could hardly have done it better than he did in this psalm. Set the works side by side and they read like a conversation between two troubled friends.

Job: The Lord gave, and the Lord has taken away; blessed be the name of the Lord.[68]

David: Yes! Bless the Lord, O my soul, and all that is within me, bless His holy name.

Job: Have you ever thought about the futility of life? Men live and die in an instant. Between morning and evening they are destroyed; they perish forever without any regarding it. Their tent-cord is plucked up within them, and they die devoid of wisdom. My days are

---

68. The words of Job in this conversation are from the following verses: Job 1:20; 4:20–21; 9:25–26; 14:1–2; 7:16–18; 13:24–25; 19:9; 14:18–21; 10:8–9; 16:12–13; 7:7–10; 10:20–21; 14:18–19; 17:11, 19:10; 7:20–21; 10:14; 13:26; 28:28.

swifter than a runner; they flee away; they see no good. They go by like skiffs of reed, like an eagle swooping on the prey. A mortal, born of woman, few of days and full of trouble, comes up like a flower and withers, flees like a shadow and does not last.

David: Exactly. As for mortals, their days are like grass; they flourish like a flower of the field; for the wind passes over it, and it is gone, and its place knows it no more.

Job: Why doesn't God leave us alone? I loathe my life; I would not live forever. Let me alone, for my days are a breath. What are human beings, that you make so much of them, that you set your mind on them, visit them every morning, test them every moment? Why do you hide your face and count me as your enemy? Will you frighten a windblown leaf and pursue dry chaff?

David: It may not feel like it to you now, but the reason God doesn't leave you alone is because He loves you. As a father has compassion on his children, so the Lord has compassion for those who fear Him.

Job: He has stripped my glory from me and taken the crown from my head.

David: Your crown is still there. He redeems your life from the pit and crowns you with steadfast love and mercy.

Job: The hope of men is destroyed like crumbling rock. Their children come to honor, and they do not know it; they are brought low, and it goes unnoticed.

David: Your hope and posterity are not destroyed. His righteousness is to children's children, to those who keep His covenant and remember to do His commandments.

Job: Will God forget I'm only human? Why are you so rough with me, God? Remember that you fashioned me like clay; and will you turn me to dust again? I was at ease, and He broke me in two; He seized me by the neck and dashed me to pieces; He set me up as His target; His archers surround me.

David: No, you don't see it now, but God is above all things gentle. He knows how we were made; He remembers that we are dust.

Job: Will you turn me to dust again, God? Will you destroy my future? Remember that my life is a breath; my eye will never again see good. As the cloud fades and vanishes, so those who go down to Sheol do not come up; they return no more to their houses, nor do their places know them any more. Are not the days of my life few? Let me alone, that I may find a little comfort before I go, never to return, to the land of gloom and deep darkness, the land of gloom and chaos, where light is like darkness. But the mountain falls and crumbles away, and the rock is removed from its place; the waters wear away the stones; the torrents wash away the soil of the earth; so you destroy the hope of mortals. My days are past, my plans are broken off, the desires of my heart. He has uprooted my hope like a tree.

David: God has an eternal plan for you. The steadfast love of the Lord is from everlasting to everlasting.

Job: Why don't you just forgive me, God? If I sin, what do I do to you, you watcher of humanity? Why have you made me your target? Why have I become a burden to you? Why do you not pardon my transgression and take away my iniquity? If I sin, you watch me and do not acquit me of my iniquity. For you write bitter things against me and make me reap the iniquities of my youth.

David: God does forgive you, and more abundantly than you could desire. The Lord is merciful and gracious, slow to anger and abounding in steadfast love. He will not always accuse, nor will He keep His anger forever. He does not deal with us according to our sins nor repay us according to our iniquities.

Job: I don't know the answers . . . but whatever they are, they must start with the fear of the Lord. Truly, the fear of the Lord, that is wisdom; and to depart from evil is understanding.

David: Yes, the fear of the Lord is the answer. His steadfast love is great toward those who fear Him. He has compassion for those who fear Him; His steadfast love is from everlasting to everlasting on those who fear Him.

~~~

The difference between the perspectives of Job and David might be more the result of timing than of superior wisdom. Job asked his questions in the midst of his troubles, and David answers them perhaps after he's seen at least the beginning of God's deliverance. Job is seated on the ash heap; David has gotten up and begun to brush himself off. Job is still at the bottom of the pit from which David has escaped.

They come in the end, though, to the same conclusion: We can bless God regardless of our circumstances, even when we cannot understand His ways. The God of creation cares about what He has made, and He is worthy of our trust and our reverent fear; we are safe in His hands.

CHAPTER 10

MAIMED BY GOD: WRESTLING, GROANING, BLESSING

I HURT MY BACK ON THE DAY ALLISON DIED. ALLI was not a particularly large girl, but neither was she tiny, and as I moved her unconscious body from the house to the car—or perhaps from the car into the hospital—I threw my back out for the first time in my life. A little while later, as Jodi and I awaited word on Allison in the emergency ward hall, a nurse came and told us she had a more comfortable place for us to wait. Jodi stood up and followed her around the corner; several seconds later, their heads popped around the corner to see where I was. I was sitting right where they left me; I couldn't get up without help.

My back hurt through the next few days, through the haze of the memorial service and visits from friends and family. It forced me to sit and think, which didn't seem a blessing at first—I wanted to get out of the house, yell, run until I was too exhausted to think—but probably was good for me in the long run.

A year later, I threw my back out again, this time helping friends move a couch up three flights of stairs.

And then a couple of months ago I hurt it again, brushing my teeth. No, worse than that. I hurt it *after* brushing my teeth. I put my toothbrush back in its place on the shelf, turned to go back into the bedroom, and found suddenly that I couldn't move.

I was in bed for five days, almost totally immobile. On the third or fourth day, I found that if someone helped me up, I could get myself to the bathroom by falling forward until my hands hit the wall and then following the wall around the room to the door. It was a full month before I was back to something close to normal.

And in each of those incidents, despite the inconvenience, I barely minded the pain at all. In fact, a week after the first injury, when my back started feeling better, I was even a little disappointed. Because the back pain reminded me of Allison; it was her last gift to me. Her life and death have changed my life forever, and it seems right that I carry a physical reminder of her with me.

I imagine Jacob felt the same way about his limp after his struggle with God.

The curious story of Jacob's wrestling match with God is found in Genesis, the first book of the Bible. Jacob is returning home after spending many years in a distant country. He is in desperate straits, alone and worried and unable to handle the events of his life. His brother Esau, who swore years before that he would kill him, is coming to meet Jacob the next day. That night "a man" wrestles with Jacob until daybreak, and though the man puts Jacob's hip out of joint, Jacob refuses to let him go until the man blesses him. The man finally does bless Jacob and changes his name to Israel. Jacob comments, "I have seen God face to face, and yet my life is preserved."[69] It's a strange and mysterious event, and Jacob himself would probably have wondered the next day if it had been a dream—if it weren't for the limp with which he awoke.

---

69. Genesis 32:22–32

What a luxury to awake with a limp, to be maimed by God—to carry a constant, physical reminder of His touch, a reminder never to allow things to return to normal. Something to slow you down when you want to run ahead, to remind you of the futility of fighting and of your inability to accomplish anything through hurry and scheming and brute strength. A new physical characteristic to accompany your new identity and your new faith.

I don't wake up with back pain every day, but the grief is always there. I wouldn't do away with it if I could. It reminds me of God's touch; it reminds me of Allison. It hurts, but it's a hurt I can live with. It's a hurt that I *need* to live with.

THE WOUND IS NO LONGER RAW. But it has not disappeared. That is as it should be. If he was worth loving, he was worth grieving over. Grief is existential testimony to the worth of the one loved. That worth abides.

So I own my grief. I do not try to put it behind me, to get over it, to forget it. I do not try to *dis*-own it. If someone asks, "Who are you, tell me about yourself," I say—not immediately, but shortly—"I am one who lost a son." That loss determines my identity—not all of my identity, but much of it. It belongs within my story. I struggle indeed to go beyond merely owning my grief toward owning it *redemptively*. But I will not and cannot disown it. I shall remember Eric. Lament is part of life.

Nicholas Wolterstorff, *Lament for a Son*

I HAVE MET SO MANY people who were never really blessed until they strove against God, were wounded, were given both a new identity and a haunting question, and who discovered in the most unlikely place, the most unexpected face—the face of God. These are people who never really danced until they limped. They are people whose self-reliance has been shattered, who have wrestled with *the man*, and who have found Him both brusque and embracing, wounding and blessing, and always stronger than they are. Not safe. But good.

Mark Buchanan, *Your God Is Too Safe*

SORROW TOOK UP PERMANENT residence in my soul and enlarged it.

Jerry Sittser, *A Grace Disguised*

Like Jacob, our family has wrestled with God—not good-natured rough-and-tumble horseplay between friends, but an exhausting, desperate struggle. Is He really there? Will He show himself? Will He show himself to be good? The struggle didn't last long; the answers to all those questions turned out to be yes.

I'm afraid I have not done a good job explaining how we came to that conclusion or describing the depth of the peace God has given us. I'm not sure, though, that that's entirely my fault; I think perhaps that the most vital element of God's comfort is inexpressible. If you make a list of all the facts and lessons I learned from Job, Moses, Paul, and David, they'll add up to far less than the actual comfort I received. That's because the comfort comes from the experience of God's presence, not from the construction of a doctrine.

For us, as for many others, a deepening awareness of God's presence began with a struggle. That struggle has transformed our lives; we know God better and depend on ourselves less. But we have not yet arrived at our final destination; though our struggle with God ended quickly, many others continue.

We believe that our lives are secure in God's hands, yet we are still sometimes accosted by sudden fears. Backing the car into the garage, we jam on the brakes and our hearts begin to pound. Where's Andrea? Could she have wandered into the garage? The kids are half an hour late coming home. Have they been in an accident? Will we ever see them alive again? A lingering illness in one of the kids, a mysterious and persistent pain—could it be cancer? We're waiting for the other shoe to drop; we know there's no reason why it shouldn't.

What those who have suffered loss understand is that these fears are not irrational. We know that a 99.9-percent survival rate means a devastating loss for one family out of a thousand, and that your love for God is no guarantee against that one family being yours. We come up against the indisputable conclusion that the faith we were resting in before was based largely not on the providence of God but on statistics.

This is a humbling and disconcerting realization. But it's a blessing, too, the time of questioning that catastrophic loss brings. Our faith needed to be questioned. Allison's death was like a flood that tests the foundations of a house; it showed us where the foundation was firm and washed away the rest. Now we're struggling to rebuild. We want to take our time and build a foundation out of lasting truths, not just patch it up with bits of the old wreckage. The new foundation must offer peace in the midst of the storm, not just a blind hope that the storm won't hit.

"Don't doubt in the dark what you've learned in the light," they say. What they don't tell you is that life's vital lessons aren't learned in the light at all, but in the darkest pit. Like Jacob, I have been given a new identity: everything I know about God, I know from the perspective of a father who has lost a daughter. This, as it turns out, is a helpful perspective from which to view the Bible, because the God we worship is also a father who suffered the death a child. I dare not forget in the light what I've learned in the dark.

Like countless others who have suffered loss, I've received a gift—the sudden, clear, accurate realization that something is vitally wrong with this world. Our lives, like so many things in this world, are transitory; without God's ultimate meaning, there is no meaning. Creation is groaning, says Paul, subjected to futility, eagerly longing for God to straighten things out. An adequate theology will not avoid this truth but embrace it. As Mark Buchanan writes, we must "learn to join our groaning, pitch for pitch and rhythm for rhythm, to the groaning of all creation . . . Groaning is creation's song, the blues of the cosmos, and we're to hum its melody and take up its chorus."[70]

⌒

We struggle to deal with the hole left in our lives by Allison's death. This battle is constant, though it changes shape from month to month, from year to year. Recently I came into our bedroom and found Nicky with Jodi on our bed, looking at pictures of Allison. Nicky was holding tight to the felt pillow of Alli's he had given us two years before. Suddenly he burst into tears; "I just wish we had more time with her," he said. We cried with him. "I know Allison is with Jesus," he said. "But I'm not always sure. Sometimes I wonder if any of it's true." When he left the room, he took Alli's pillow with him.

We think about Allison daily, hourly. We often pray that God would give her a hug for us. I would give anything to have her back for just five minutes—to tell her what she means to me, to give her a long hug, to laugh with her. For those five minutes I would gladly give twenty years of my life. Nobody's offering, of course. And then again, I wouldn't want to give away any of

---

70. *Things Unseen* (Sisters, OR: Multnomah Press, 2002), 10–11.

the time I have left with my other children, who are themselves more important to me than ever before. Besides, I don't know that I have twenty years left of my life to trade—or two minutes, for that matter. There are no guarantees on that subject. This is one truth that we've learned in the hardest way possible.

We know life will never be the same; Allison is not coming back; things will never return to normal. This is hard, and yet, who would want things to return to normal, anyway? We'd love to have Allison back, yes. We look back now on our days with her the way a man with toothache or cancer yearns for the days of his health. But Alli will never return, and nothing else about the "normal" holds any appeal for us. Allison's death taught us what was wrong about our life: our hurrying, our shuffled priorities, the lack of family fun time and healthy hugs, the ease with which we goad each other and the infrequency with which we encourage. The loss of Allison brought us many tears, but it also made us—at least for little while—pay more attention to things that are really important. We hugged each other more and were more careful to give voice to our feelings. We were more considerate of others, more sympathetic to their pain, and because of our loss were allowed deeper entrance into their lives. We had more to say and didn't have to raise our voices to say it. Our family was at once both fragile and powerful.

◦━

We struggle to hold on to those lessons. Sadly, incredibly, they tend to slip away. I can offer only one proof that I have been changed forever: since Allison's death, I never, ever hurry through a hug. That's not an insignificant detail, but I admit that I had hoped by now to have seen many other permanent changes.

In the days following Allison's death, I told myself I would never again waste my time puttering around, doing busy work, answering unimportant e-mails, or whatever it is I do on the computer all day. But disappointingly quickly, I found myself involved in the same meaningless activities. When Alli died, I discovered in myself a new patience with others; I found I could give them room to grow, wait for them as God had always waited for and helped me. That newfound generosity lasted, I'm afraid, about a week.

This is a hard thing to see in yourself. "We are dismayed," it has been noted, "when we find that even disaster cannot cure us of our faults."[71] I was indeed dismayed to notice reappearing in myself qualities I had thought dead—impatience, laziness, self-ishness, pettiness. *If I'm not changed after all we've gone through,* I thought, *when will I ever be?*

But I have changed, of course, just not as quickly and com-pletely as I had hoped. The transformation is an accomplished fact, but it's also a process. The antidote has been injected into a vein, but it hasn't reached every part of the body yet. Some days it's hard for us not to be impatient with ourselves for slowing down the process, for clinging to old habits.

We struggle to form new habits that better reflect our new goals, to live by a new set of priorities. We're more careful now about what we'll commit ourselves to, more deliberate in set-ting aside time for our family. It's possible that at times we've been overly vigorous in pruning back our schedule, but that's a risk we're willing to take. The risk we can't afford is that of fall-ing back into the old routines, of letting our days get choked by attractive but ultimately unfruitful activities.

⌒

While the changes our family has undergone have been over-whelmingly positive, I'd be lying if I said we're always easier to get along with than we used to be. Because while Alli's death has

---

71. Luc de Clapiers, the marquis de Vauvenargues

given us more patience with those who disagree with us, it has also left us with a greater impatience with petty disputes; and with our new desire to pursue life's important matters comes a corresponding irritation at having our time wasted. Like everyone else, we struggle to find a balance. I hope what I've gone through has pushed me closer to the side of patience, tolerance, and forgiveness, but I can't honestly say that is always the case.

What I can say is that we are making progress—sometimes barely perceptible, and accompanied with frequent setbacks—but progress nonetheless. And I have the sense that we are moving in the right direction, toward becoming the family and the individuals we want to be. We've endeavored to align ourselves with God's purposes, and we're starting to see that to the extent we did that, we were aligning ourselves with our own best good. In blessing God, we were blessing ourselves.

And so like David, we end where we began—by blessing the Lord.

> The Lord has established his throne in the heavens,
>   and his kingdom rules over all.
> Bless the Lord, O you his angels,
>   you mighty ones who do his bidding,
>   obedient to his spoken word.
> Bless the Lord, all his hosts,
>   his ministers that do his will.
> Bless the Lord, all his works,
>   in all places of his dominion.
> Bless the Lord, O my soul (Psalm 103:19–22).

Though David has come full circle, he is miles from his starting point. The psalm that began as a subdued solo ends in triumph, in a mighty chorus of angels and of creation itself. "One lonely soul on fire with the love of God may set the whole universe ablaze,"[72] writes F. B. Meyer, perhaps missing the fact that the universe is already ablaze.

> The heavens are telling the glory of God;
>   and the firmament proclaims his handiwork.
> Day to day pours forth speech,
>   and night to night declares knowledge,
>   sings David in Psalm 19:1–2.

"Join in the chorus," David is urging himself, with an implicit invitation to us as well. "God is in charge, and heaven and earth are singing His praises. Don't be left behind; join in His praise; bless the Lord."

Yes, like our own lives, creation reflects God's glory somewhat dimly. The flower fades; our lives are touched by sorrow. The world is broken. As David found, though, the existence of sorrow does not have to dampen joy. Our fragility motivates us to rejoice in His permanence; our weakness in His strength; our sin in His forgiveness.

There is tremendous advantage to us in answering David's call to praise; blessing God opens up our broken lives to God's blessing. As Alexander Maclaren points out, though, there's another good reason to join the chorus: the chorus needs our voice.

> From ver. 19 to the end, the psalm takes a still wider sweep. It now embraces the universe. But it is noticeable that there is no more about "lovingkindness" in these verses. Man's sin and frailty make him a fit recipient of it, but we do not know that in all creation another being capable of and needing it is found . . .

---

72. *F. B. Meyer on the Psalms* (Grand Rapids: Zondervan), 125.

That "choir invisible" praises the King of heaven; but later revelation has taught us that men shall teach a new song to "principalities and powers in heavenly places," because only men can praise Him whose lovingkindness to them, sinful and dying, redeemed them by His blood . . .

Nature and angels, stars and suns, seas and forests, magnify their Maker and Sustainer; we alone can bless the God who pardons iniquities and heals diseases which our fellow-choristers never knew.[73]

This is an awesome truth: We can praise God in a way that creation and angels cannot. Christ did not die on the cross for the angels; the stars have never needed God's mercy, His forgiveness, or His comfort. The voice of those who are forgiven, the voice of those who suffer, the voice of those who bless God even when they're hurting, add a harmony to the heavenly chorus that would be totally absent without them.

The angels and creation cannot offer a sacrifice of praise.

I've been thinking lately about a popular chorus from a few years ago that spoke of joy as "a happiness without alloy." But I wonder now if joy is, in fact, an alloy—a happiness made both stronger and less brittle by mixing it with the element of suffering. Perhaps the furnace of pain melds as well as purifies, making possible a joy that's stronger than a mere gladness untouched by sorrow.

Jesus once told a parable about two debtors to a Pharisee named Simon:

---

73. *The Expositor's Bible*, 258–9.

"Two men owed money to a certain moneylender. One owed him five hundred denarii, and the other fifty. Neither of them had the money to pay him back, so he canceled the debts of both. Now which of them will love him more?"

Simon replied, "I suppose the one who had the bigger debt canceled."

"You have judged correctly," Jesus said (Luke 7:41–43 NIV).

I think that David experienced the great love that results from great forgiveness. It's evident that he discovered, too, the great joy that can result from great suffering. It's my prayer that my family—and families like mine—will find that great joy as well.

May the joy of our hearts be deepened and increased as we align ourselves with God's purposes.

Your will be done in us, as it is in heaven.
Bless the Lord, O my soul.

SO WE DO NOT LOSE heart. Even though our outer nature is wasting away, our inner nature is being renewed day by day. For this slight momentary affliction is preparing us for an eternal weight of glory beyond all measure, because we look not at what can be seen but at what cannot be seen; for what can be seen is temporary, but what cannot be seen is eternal.

2 Corinthians 4:16–18

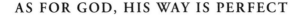

AS FOR GOD, HIS WAY IS PERFECT

He alone is just
It's not time to question now
But look to Him with trust.

Lord, you give, and take away
We will thank You when we pray
We know now that Allison
Is by your side, and with your Son.

Father, You're so merciful
To be with us right here
We could not endure this pain
Without your presence near

We'll miss Alli, we will cry
But we will see her when we die
Until then, and through the tears
We'll thank You for her thirteen years.

—At age fifteen, Nate (Allison's brother)
wrote this poem for Allison's memorial service

A BLESSING FOR YOU

The Lord bless you and keep you;
 the Lord make his face to shine upon you, and be
  gracious to you;
 the Lord lift up his countenance upon you, and
  give you peace.

Numbers 6:24–26

AND AN INVITATION

In Ezekiel 47:6–10, Ezekiel describes his vision of the temple in the New Jerusalem, where he is given a tour by a man whose appearance shines like bronze:

> He said to me, "Mortal, have you seen this?"
> Then he led me back along the bank of the river. As I came back, I saw on the bank of the river a great many trees on one side and on the other. He said to me, "This water flows toward the eastern region and goes down into the Arabah; and when it enters the sea, the sea of stagnant waters, the water will become fresh. Wherever the river goes, every living creature that swarms will live, and there will be very many fish, once these waters reach there. It will become fresh; and everything will live where the river goes. People will stand fishing beside the sea from En-gedi to En-eglaim; it will be a place for the spreading of nets; its fish will be of a great many kinds, like the fish of the Great Sea.

You can look for me fishing there, with Allison. There will be lots of friends and family with us, and we will all be in the presence of our Father, our guide.

You're welcome to join us. There will be plenty of room, plenty of fish, and plenty of time. It would give us great joy to see you there.

Note to the Reader

THE PUBLISHER INVITES YOU TO SHARE YOUR RESPONSE to the message of this book by writing Discovery House Publishers, P.O. Box 3566, Grand Rapids, MI 49501, U.S.A. For information about other Discovery House books, music, videos, or DVDs, contact us at the same address or call 1-800-653-8333. Find us on the Internet at http://www.dhp.org/ or send an e-mail to books@dhp.org.